ICT Matters 1

TEACHER BOOK

Liz Hankin • David Sutton • David Dunn

www.heinemann.co.uk
✓ Free online support
✓ Useful weblinks
✓ 24 hour online ordering

01865 888058

Inspiring generations

Heinemann Educational Publishers
Halley Court, Jordan Hill, Oxford OX2 8EJ
Part of Harcourt Education

Heinemann is the registered trademark of
Harcourt Education Limited
© *Liz Hankin, David Sutton, David Dunn 2003*

First published 2003

08 07 06 05 04 03
10 9 8 7 6 5 4 3 2 1

British Library Cataloguing in Publication Data is available from the British Library
on request.

ISBN 0 435 10840 9

Cover design by Hicksdesign
Cover photo: © Powerstock

Designed by Wooden Ark Studio
Produced by Kamae Design
Printed in the UK by Athenaeum Press

Acknowledgements
Every effort has been made to contact copyright holders of material reproduced
in this book. Any omissions will be rectified in subsequent printings if notice is
given to the publishers.

Cadbury's logo and screengrab. Reproduced with kind permission of Cadbury's UK; Screengrab from
www.virginmobile.com/mobile. Reprinted with the kind permission of Virgin; Advert from Clarks 'Life's One
Long Catwalk' campaign. Reprinted with the kind permission of C & J Clark International Limited; Egg.com logo.
Reprinted with the kind permission of Egg.com PR Team; Smile.co.uk logo. Reprinted with the kind permission of
Smile, Marketing; Goldfish logo. Reprinted with the kind permission of Centrica UK; Lloyds TSB logo.
Reproduced with kind permission of Lloyds TSB Corporate; Penguin logo. Reprinted with the kind permission of
Penguin UK; Fat Face logo. Reproduced with kind permission of Fat Face; Walkers Crisps logo. Reproduced with
kind permission of Stuart Higgins on behalf of Walkers; Mc V logo. Reproduced with kind permission of United
Biscuits; WWF logo. Reproduced with kind permission of WWF-UK; 'Population Projections for 2025-2050' from
www.prb.org. Reprinted by permission of PRB (Population Reference Bureau); Litter picking by William Heath
Robinson. Reproduced by permission of Pollinger Limited and the Estate of Mrs. J. C. Robinson; 'How to keep
shop windows clean' by Rube Goldberg. Rube Goldberg is the ® and © of Rube Goldberg Inc. Reproduced with
the kind permission of Rube Goldberg Inc.; Elodea data © Science at Clifton College.

Photographs: Do Not Enter road sign: Photodisc; Piltdown man hoax: Rex Features; English fields: Alamy;
Hills: Alamy; Garden in spring: Harcourt Index/Corbis; Highrise flats: Rex Features; Food: Harcourt Index/Corbis;
Oranges: Harcourt Index/Corbis; Mobile phone (text message): Peter Morris; Door lock: Alamy.

Illustrations: Castle map: Louise Curphey

Video footage stills © David Sutton/Edicts

Contents

Introduction   **4**

Matching grid   **11**

Module 1
Creating a presentation   13

Module 2
Using data and information sources   35

Module 3
Making a leaflet   48

Module 4
Modelling and presenting numeric data   73

Module 5
Data handling   95

Module 6
Control and monitoring   117

Appendix
Data logging   140

ICT Matters
Introduction

ICT Matters is a lively, easy to use Key Stage 3 ICT course for pupils of a wide ability range. It is based on the Framework Yearly Teaching Objectives and has been carefully designed so that it can be used either as a stand-alone course, or alongside the DfES sample teaching units. It is an interactive, task-based course which supports whole class teaching and individual and group work. Skills development is integrated throughout.

The components

ICT Matters 1 consists of one Pupil Book, one Teacher Book and one Resource Bank CD ROM for each of the three years of Key Stage 3. The Pupil Book is available in two different formats:

- The Workstation edition is wiro bound so that it can be easily propped up against the monitor for use in the ICT suite.
- The Desk edition is sewn paperback and is ideal for use in the classroom or for homework.

Pupil Book

The Pupil Books are divided into 6 modules, which are sub-divided into a number of units which deliver all the knowledge, skills and understanding required.

Each module begins with 2–3 pages called Prior learning which provides support for transition from KS2. For more information on this, see the section on Transition on page 5.

Each unit starts with a clear statement of its learning objective. Content is interspersed with tasks which are differentiated by use of colour coding. Green tasks can be tackled by all pupils, and most should be able to complete them. Red tasks are more difficult and are designed to extend more able students. They are likely to require either more advanced skills or more complex and integrated thinking, or both. For the most able pupils there is also an additional extension task for each unit provided in the Teacher Book.

Running through each module is a Module Task which is like a mini-project. Pupils complete the Module Task with help and instruction as they go along. They may work on it individually, in pairs or in a larger group.

At the end of each module is an Assignment which draws together all the learning in the module. It is expected that pupils will work on an assignment largely unaided, thus providing a way of checking how far pupils have really assimilated the learning from the module. The assignments can also be used as a tool for assessing NC levels. For more information on this, see the additional notes on Assessment on page 6.

At the end of each module there is a Skills help section, identified by a pale blue tint background. These pages provide step-by-step instruction, supported by screenshots, on all the software skills required to carry out the tasks in the module.

A Glossary at the end of the book gives simple definitions for all key vocabulary used.

Teacher Book

The Teacher Book contains:

- Mapping grid with the Framework Yearly Teaching Objectives, the National Curriculum Programme of Study, the QCA Scheme of Work and the DfES sample teaching units.
- Guidance on assessment.
- Overview grids for each module.
- Clear teaching notes for each unit including suggested starters and extension activities for the most able students.
- Suggestions for how to use the tasks with pupils of different abilities.

Resource Bank

The Resource Bank is a CD ROM containing:

- All the electronic resources needed to do the tasks in the Pupil Book.
- Worked examples of some of the tasks.

- Video clips.
- Presentation and Lesson objectives slides.
- A bank of image and sound files for pupils to use in their own work.
- Information sheets and Worksheets* to support many of the tasks.
- Additional Skills Helpsheets* covering more advanced skills.

*All Worksheets, Information sheets and Helpsheets are available in pdf format and in MS Word so that you can customise them if you wish.

Teaching the course

The teaching sequence

The modules can be taught in any order, but it is generally not advisable to change the order of units within a module because the module tasks build up over the units. Generally a unit equates to a lesson, but some schools may wish to take a longer or shorter time to cover particular units.

In the Year 7 Pupil Book the modules and units correspond closely to the DfES sample teaching units. As the course progresses through Years 8 and 9 there is more flexibility in the structure to allow for progression and more project-based teaching. However, all the materials for Years 7, 8 and 9 are cross-referenced to the sample teaching units in detail so that they can be used alongside them, if desired.

Transition

In the Year 7 Pupil Book only, each module begins with a Prior learning section which identifies the Knowledge, Skills and Understanding which pupils should be bringing with them from KS2. Short sections of information, plus a skills-based task, help pupils and teachers to identify areas which require catch-up work or reinforcement.

Differentiation

Colour coded differentiated tasks are provided throughout the Pupil Book. In addition, the teacher notes for the tasks often provide guidance on how to differentiate by outcome, and on how to modify tasks to make them suitable for more- or less-able pupils. Many of the tasks require pupils to work with partners or in groups, giving opportunities for differentiated working on the same task.

Cross-curricular themes

This course purposely focuses on ICT as a stand-alone subject. However, there is a section at the end of each Module Overview which identifies possible opportunities for cross-curricular teaching or application of learning.

Collaborative working

ICT Matters provides numerous opportunities for pupils to work together on tasks. Throughout the modules there are examples of whole class, group, paired and individual task work.

- Whole class activities have been used as an introduction to a new concept, a stage of a process or within a plenary session.
- Group activities have been indicated as different starter activities.
- Working with a partner has been used throughout the modules to provide the opportunity for pupils to reflect upon their outcomes in comparison with those of others and also as a tool where they need to experiment, research or try out new procedures.

The different methods of working will enable differentiated activities to be added into a lesson. Teachers may choose to make use of tasks to provide peer support by mixing pupils with different levels of ability or to test and extend pupils with higher ability to progress further.

Paired work will also maximise the use of resources. Although each pupil will usually be expected to produce their own version of a task, they could share resources and work collaboratively to achieve this.

Where collaborative working has taken place with pupils producing a joint outcome, pupils should annotate the work to demonstrate their contributions.

Assessment

Portfolio building

Pupils need to be made aware that they will be building a portfolio. Their portfolio will remind them how to make use of ICT tools and techniques as well as demonstrate their achievement.

To make full use of their portfolios pupils will need to:

- Keep draft copies of their work where the copies are part of a process.
- Annotate their work as they are working. The annotations should indicate why they made decisions as well their own 'tips' about what they physically did to produce items.
- Keep their portfolio in the logical order of tasks and activities and make use of relevant file names that will assist them in knowing what the content of a file is.

As the electronic version of their portfolio increases, teachers may choose to archive the pupil files to a CD-ROM or other storage media. This could provide a useful backup version as evidence of achievement.

Assessment for learning

Shared goals and outcomes

Learning objectives are clearly indicated at the beginning of each unit and module and are introduced prior to tasks being undertaken.

The learning objectives follow the ICT Key Stage 3 strategy.

Peer group assessment

Pupils have opportunities throughout the modules to support and carry out evaluation of their own and other pupils' work.

Formative assessment

Before tackling a module pupils can use the Prior learning section to establish their own level of skills and knowledge against those needed to complete the first stages of a module. They can see what the objectives are for the module and seek support for the areas where they feel weak.

The plenary sessions at the end of each unit enable discussion about outcome and methods of improvement.

In addition, pupils complete an evaluation sheet at the end of each module assignment that will help them to reflect upon areas where they have improved and where they might need on-going support.

Summative assessment

To make use of *ICT Matters* to carry out formal assessment of pupil achievement, teachers can use the tasks within each unit and the module Assignments.

Using the module assignments

After a pupil has completed the units within a module they can test out the skills and knowledge they have acquired by completing the assignment. It should be possible to complete most Assignments within a 60-minute session but it may be necessary to spread some over two sessions, for example to allow pupils time to collect data. Not all pupils have to complete the assignment at the same time.

Self-evaluation form

There is an evaluation form provided on the CD ROM for each module that pupils should complete after they have concluded the work on the units and the assignment within a module. They should be given a copy of the form before thay start the assignment so they can see what they should be able to achieve.

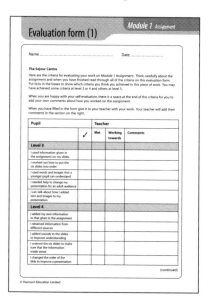

They are asked to make judgements about the criteria that they have met and make comments about carrying out the assignment.

After they have completed the form they will hand it to you for you to discuss and provide feedback (verbal or written), including an NC level if appropriate.

Pupils may require assistance at first in making judgements. It would be appropriate to carry out a dry run, explaining the evaluation criteria for the first assignment completed, to assist the pupils in making their decisions.

Awarding levels

To be awarded a level for an assignment, pupils should be demonstrating that they have met all of the criteria for that level. To be working towards a level, pupils should be demonstrating that they have either met, or are working towards all of the criteria for that level.

NB They may also have met or be working towards higher levels on some criteria.

The exemplar grid below gives some possible scenarios and suggested levels which could be awarded.

Met			Working towards			Suggested level
3	4	5	3	4	5	
None	None	None	Some	None	None	Below L3
Some	None	None	Some	None	None	Below L3
Some	None	None	Rest	Some	None	WT L3
All	Some	None		Some	None	Level 3
All	Some	None		Some	Some	Level 3
All	Some	None		Rest	Some	WT L4
All	All	None			Some	L4
All	All	Some			Some	L4
All	All	Some			Rest	WT L5
All	All	All				L5 or more

Key

Met

All = has met all the criteria at that level
Some = has met some of the criteria at that level
None = has met none of the criteria at that level

Working towards

All = is working towards all the criteria at that level
Some = is working towards some of the criteria at that level
Rest = is working towards all the criteria at that level which have not yet been met
None = is not working towards any of the criteria at that level

Technical issues

It is expected that schools will want to copy the files from the Resource Bank CD ROM onto their school network so that they are easily accessible to pupils and teachers. The file structure on the CD ROM is reproduced on pages 9–10 for your reference.

Some files which are only for teacher use have been stored in a separate directory called *Teacher-Only Resources*, so that they can be easily saved to a staff-only area of the network.

The Internet

All the hotlinks mentioned in the course are accessed via the Heinemann website. The links are checked regularly and if one goes down, an appropriate replacement link is created as quickly as possible.

It is assumed that schools will have a policy regarding Internet safety which will be covered with pupils early in KS3, and certainly before they tackle Module 2.

Using the electronic resources

Network areas

In many tasks pupils are asked to open a file from the Resource Bank, work on it and then save it with their own filename. We recommend that if you copy the files from the CD to your hard drive or network, you set the file as read-only, so pupils have to save the file with a new name before any changes can be made. You will need to set up a directory for each pupil where they can store their work. In addition there needs to be a shared area where all pupils in a class can access and store shared files. Basic information has been given about working on a network, but you will need to cover this in some detail with your Year 7 pupils when they first arrive, in order to ensure that they are familiar with how to use your particular network.

File naming

Many of the tasks are cumulative and it is important that pupils keep versions of their work as they go along. You may want to suggest that they always use a convention, such as putting v1, v2 etc. at the end of a filename, so that they can track the progress of their work.

Worksheets

Many of the tasks have associated Worksheets on which pupils can write their answers. If you prefer, pupils can write their answers in their exercise books. Where a worksheet is available, it is indicated in the Task Notes in this Teacher Book.

Some of the Worksheets are designed so that they can be completed electronically. All the electronic resources are stored as read-only files so that pupils are forced to make a copy before they work on them.

Printing

Some of the tasks ask pupils to print out their work in order to annotate it or share it with others. You will probably want to set some rules about how, when and where pupils print. There is a note in the introduction of the Pupil Book emphasising that pupils should always ask the teacher before printing anything.

Email

Use of email is a teaching objective from Year 7 onwards. Whilst many pupils will already be regular users of email when they come into KS3, there are many schools which do not yet have the infrastructure to support pupil email on a large scale. None of the tasks in the Pupil Book specifically require the use of email, but teachers in schools which do support pupil email may wish to suggest, for example, that pupils email a file home to work on it for homework, rather than printing it out.

Downloading images

You may prefer to tell your pupils to use **Save As** and **Import File** rather than **Copy and Paste** when inserting images into documents, as the files may then take up less space. Pupils will also need guidance as to the preferred format for saving images into different document types. For example, .jpg files sometimes make Word documents very large. All images on the Resource Bank CD ROM are saved as .jpg files.

Images from the Internet

Pupils may import images from the Internet into their documents, but it should be stressed to them that they can only use images which are copyright free.

Software

General

All electronic files and all Skills help sections in *ICT Matters* are created using Microsoft Office 2000 products. The electronic files should be capable of being opened in any later version of MS software. Some of the instructions in the Skills help sections may vary slightly with different versions of the software, but the same options are nearly always available, even if presented slightly differently.

Databases

In Module 5 of *ICT Matters 1*, MS Excel rather than Access is used to create a data handling structure. Simple queries are done using sorting and filtering. Pupils are introduced to the basic structure of a database and the basic concepts of running a query, without having to deal with the rigours of a very powerful and complex database package. As pupils start to work with more complex data structures and queries in Years 8 and 9, Access will be introduced.

File structure for Resource Bank CD ROM

Folder	Subfolder	Files			
Appendix – Data logging		Resource Pondweed.xls			
Image bank		Aeroplane.jpg Autumn.jpg Ballet dancer.jpg Big top.jpg Cakes.jpg Canoeing.jpg Cat.jpg Chorus line dancers.jpg Clouds.jpg Clown 1.jpg Clown 2.jpg Clowns.jpg Club dancefloor.jpg	Dinosaur.jpg Dog.jpg English beach.jpg English hills.jpg English wood.jpg Festival.jpg Football fans.jpg Football players.jpg Goldfish.jpg Hamster.jpg Horse riding.jpg Horse.jpg Hotdog.jpg	Juggler on highwire.jpg Juggler.jpg Kitten.jpg Lions.jpg Performing horses.jpg Playground.jpg Puppy.jpg Rabbit.jpg Rat.jpg Seal.jpg Skyscrapers.jpg Space shuttle.jpg Spring.jpg	Stormclouds.jpg Summer.jpg Sunrise.jpg Sunset.jpg Swimming pool.jpg Teenagers 1.jpg Teenagers 2.jpg The Alps.jpg Trapeze artists.jpg Tropical beach.jpg Tropical rainforest.jpg Winter.jpg	
Module 1	Electronic Resources	Resource 1 Mico's circus.ppt Resource 1.1 My pets.ppt Resource 1.1 School information 1.ppt Resource 1.1 School information 2.ppt Resource 1.2 Formats.ppt Resource 1.2 Images.ppt Resource 1.2 School information 3.ppt	Resource 1.2 School information 4.ppt Resource 1.3 Colours.ppt Resource 1.3 Fonts.ppt Resource 1.3 Order.ppt Resource 1.4 Sounds.ppt Resource 1.6 Transitions.ppt		
	Lesson Objectives	Unit 1.1 Lesson Objectives.ppt Unit 1.2 Lesson Objectives.ppt	Unit 1.3 Lesson Objectives.ppt Unit 1.4 Lesson Objectives.ppt	Unit 1.5 Lesson Objectives.ppt Unit 1.6 Lesson Objectives.ppt	
	Worksheets	Module 1 Evaluation form.doc Module 1 Evaluation form.pdf Resource 1.2 What's it for.doc Resource 1.2 What's it for.pdf Resource 1.3 Font puzzles.doc Resource 1.3 Font puzzles.pdf Resource 1.4 Sound sense.doc Resource 1.4 Sound sense.pdf Resource 1.4 Sounds like what.doc	Resource 1.4 Sounds like what.pdf Resource 1.4 TV sound log.doc Resource 1.4 TV sound log.pdf Resource 1.5 Performance checklist.doc Resource 1.5 Performance checklist.pdf Resource 1.6 Content checklist.doc Resource 1.6 Content checklist.pdf Resource 1.6 Evaluation list.doc Resource 1.6 Evaluation list.pdf		
Module 2	Electronic Resources	Resource 2.1 Cats.ppt Resource 2.1 Holidays.ppt	Resource 2.3 What it says.ppt Resource 2.3 Words.ppt		
	Lesson Objectives	Unit 2.1 Lesson Objectives.ppt	Unit 2.2 Lesson Objectives.ppt	Unit 2.3 Lesson Objectives.ppt	
	Worksheets	Module 2 Assignment worksheet.doc Module 2 Assignment worksheet.pdf Module 2 Evaluation form.doc Module 2 Evaluation form.pdf Resource 2.1 Questions.doc Resource 2.1 Questions.pdf Resource 2.1 Survey.doc Resource 2.1 Survey.pdf	Resource 2.2 Sharks.doc Resource 2.2 Sharks.pdf Resource 2.2 Web page.doc Resource 2.2 Web page.pdf Resource 2.3 Comparisons.doc Resource 2.3 Comparisons.pdf Resource 2.3 Professors.doc Resource 2.3 Professors.pdf		
Module 3	Electronic Resources	Resource 3 Circus poster.doc Resource 3 Mouse.bmp Resource 3.1 Adverts.ppt Resource 3.1 Corporate.ppt Resource 3.1 Layers.pub Resource 3.1 Names.ppt	Resource 3.1 Newsletter.pub Resource 3.2 Food.bmp Resource 3.2 Good and bad.doc Resource 3.3 Places.pub Resource 3.4 Graphics.bmp Resource 3.6 Overlap.pub		
	Lesson Objectives	Unit 3.1 Lesson Objectives.ppt Unit 3.2 Lesson Objectives.ppt	Unit 3.3 Lesson Objectives.ppt Unit 3.4 Lesson Objectives.ppt	Unit 3.5 Lesson Objectives.ppt Unit 3.6 Lesson Objectives.ppt	
	Worksheets	Module 3 Evaluation form.doc Module 3 Evaluation form.pdf Resource 3.2 Plus and minus.doc Resource 3.2 Plus and minus.pdf Resource 3.3 Logos.doc Resource 3.3 Logos.pdf Resource 3.3 Vector logos.doc Resource 3.3 Vector logos.pdf Resource 3.4 Acquiring images.doc Resource 3.4 Acquiring images.pdf	Resource 3.4 Articles.doc Resource 3.4 Articles.pdf Resource 3.4 Word cards.doc Resource 3.4 Word cards.pdf Resource 3.5 Process.doc Resource 3.5 Process.pdf Resource 3.5 Quality.doc Resource 3.5 Quality.pdf Resource 3.6 Folds.doc Resource 3.6 Folds.pdf		

Folder	Subfolder	Files	
Module 4	Electronic Resources	Resource 4 Circus takings.xls Resource 4.1 Calendar.xls Resource 4.1 Extra.xls Resource 4.1 Shows.xls Resource 4.1 Sponsors.xls Resource 4.2 Groups.xls Resource 4.2 Show more.xls Resource 4.2 Updates.xls	Resource 4.2 What if.xls Resource 4.3 Day.xls Resource 4.3 Framed.xls Resource 4.3 Rules.xls Resource 4.3 Week.xls Resource 4.4 Changes.xls Resource 4.4 Expenses.xls Resource 4.5 Charts.ppt
	Lesson Objectives	Unit 4.1 Lesson Objectives.ppt Unit 4.3 Lesson Objectives.ppt Unit 4.5 Lesson Objectives.ppt Unit 4.2 Lesson Objectives.ppt Unit 4.4 Lesson Objectives.ppt	
	Worksheets	Module 4 Evaluation form.doc Module 4 Evaluation form.pdf Resource 4.1 Show stoppers.doc Resource 4.1 Show stoppers.pdf Resource 4.1 Sponsored Task Day.doc Resource 4.1 Sponsored Task Day.pdf Resource 4.1 Using absolute cell references.doc Resource 4.1 Using absolute cell references.pdf	Resource 4.2 Planning a model.doc Resource 4.2 Planning a model.pdf Resource 4.2 Sorting.doc Resource 4.2 Sorting.pdf Resource 4.3 Design.doc Resource 4.3 Design.pdf Resource 4.4 New rules.doc Resource 4.4 New rules.pdf
Module 5	Electronic Resources	Resource 5 Circus acts.xls Resource 5.1 Numbers.doc Resource 5.1 Population.xls Resource 5.2 Weather data.xls	Resource 5.4 Data in.xls Resource 5.5 Errors.ppt Resource 5.5 Trails.xls Resource 5.6 Music.ppt
	Lesson Objectives	Unit 5.1 Lesson Objectives.ppt Unit 5.3 Lesson Objectives.ppt Unit 5.5 Lesson Objectives.ppt Unit 5.2 Lesson Objectives.ppt Unit 5.4 Lesson Objectives.ppt Unit 5.6 Lesson Objectives.ppt	
	Worksheets	Module 5 Evaluation form.doc Module 5 Evaluation form.pdf Resource 5.2 Collection.doc Resource 5.2 Collection.pdf	Resource 5.2 Prove it.doc Resource 5.2 Prove it.pdf Resource 5.3 Questionnaire.doc Resource 5.3 Questionnaire.pdf
Module 6	Electronic Resources	Resource 6.1 Amazing machines.ppt Resource 6.1 Barrier 1.mpg Resource 6.1 Barrier 2.mpg Resource 6.1 Bikes.mpg Resource 6.2 How do you ....ppt Resource 6.2 Litter picking.ppt	Resource 6.2 Recipe.ppt Resource 6.3 Crossing.mpg Resource 6.4 Automated greenhouse.ppt Resource 6.4 Castle security.ppt Resource 6.4 Driving a car.ppt Resource 6.5 Light flash.ppt
	Lesson Objectives	Unit 6.1 Lesson Objectives.ppt Unit 6.3 Lesson Objectives.ppt Unit 6.5 Lesson Objectives.ppt Unit 6.2 Lesson Objectives.ppt Unit 6.4 Lesson Objectives.ppt	
	Worksheets	Module 6 Evaluation form.doc Module 6 Evaluation form.pdf Resource 6 Flowchart outline.doc Resource 6 Flowchart outline.pdf Resource 6.1 Automation.doc Resource 6.1 Automation.pdf Resource 6.1 Control in the kitchen.doc Resource 6.1 Control in the kitchen.pdf Resource 6.1 Input.doc Resource 6.1 Input.pdf Resource 6.2 Buggy.doc Resource 6.2 Buggy.pdf Resource 6.2 Flowchart planning sheet.doc Resource 6.2 Flowchart planning sheet.pdf Resource 6.2 Gum flowchart.doc Resource 6.2 Gum flowchart.pdf Resource 6.2 Instructions.doc Resource 6.2 Instructions.pdf	Resource 6.2 Inventions.doc Resource 6.2 Inventions.pdf Resource 6.2 Litter machine.doc Resource 6.2 Litter machine.pdf Resource 6.2 Sausage stroganoff.doc Resource 6.2 Sausage stroganoff.pdf Resource 6.3 Car safety.doc Resource 6.3 Car safety.pdf Resource 6.4 Automated room.doc Resource 6.4 Automated room.pdf Resource 6.4 Castle map.doc Resource 6.4 Castle map.pdf Resource 6.4 Simple procedure.doc Resource 6.4 Simple procedure.pdf Resource 6.5 Control commands.doc Resource 6.5 Control commands.pdf Resource 6.5 Pelican crossing.doc Resource 6.5 Pelican crossing.pdf
Sounds		Alarm clock.WAV Car skidding.WAV Girl laughing.WAV Seashore.WAV Applause.WAV Car starting.WAV Helicopter.WAV Thunder.WAV Baby crying.WAV Cheering.WAV Horse.WAV Traffic.WAV Birdsong.WAV Dog barking.WAV Phone.WAV Train.WAV Breaking glass.WAV Fireworks.WAV Police siren.WAV Wind howling.WAV	
Teacher-Only Resources		Module 4 worked example.xls Resource 6.2 Flowchart for picture snapping machine.doc Resource 6.2 Flowchart for picture snapping machine.pdf Resource 6.2 Flowchart for window cleaner.doc Resource 6.2 Flowchart for window cleaner.pdf Resource Pondweed worked example.xls	

Matching grid for Year 7

Framework	QCA SOW	NC POS	DfES Units	ICT Matters Unit
FINDING THINGS OUT				
Using data and information sources				
Understand that different forms of information (e.g. text, graphics, sound, numeric data and symbols) can be combined to create meaning and impact	2, 3	3a	7.2, 7.3	2.1, 3.1, 3.2, 3.3
Identify the purpose of an information source (e.g. to present facts or opinions, to advertise, publicise or entertain) and whether it is likely to be biased	2	1a, 1b	7.2, 7.5	2.1, 5.1
Identify what information is relevant to a task	2	1a, 1b	7.2, 7.5	2.1, 2.2, 5.3
Understand how someone using an information source could be misled by missing or inaccurate information	2	1b, 1c, 4b	7.2, 7.5	2.3, 5.1
Searching and selecting				
Search a variety of sources for information relevant to a task (e.g. using indexes, search techniques, navigational structures and engines)	2, 5	1b	7.2	2.2, 5.5
Narrow down a search to achieve more relevant results	2	1b, 4a	7.5, 7.2	2.2
Assess the value of information from various sources to a particular task	2	1a, 1b	7.2	2.3
Acknowledge sources of information used	2		7.2	2.3
Organising and investigating				
In an investigation:				
● design and use an appropriate data handling structure to answer questions and draw conclusions	5	1c, 2a	7.5	5.2, 5.4
● design a questionnaire or data collection sheet to provide relevant data	5	1b, 1c	7.5	5.3, 5.4
● check data efficiently for errors	5	1c, 4a	7.5	5.5
● investigate relationships between variables	5	1c, 2a, 2c	7.5	5.5, 5.6
● use software to represent data in simple graphs, charts or tables, justifying the choice of representation	5	3a, 3b	7.5	5.1, 5.2, 5.5
● derive new information from data (e.g. averages, probabilities)	5	2a	7.5	5.1
● check whether conclusions are plausible	5	1c, 4a	7.5	5.2, 5.3, 5.6
● review and amend the structure and its data to answers further questions	5	2a, 2c, 4a	7.5	5.6
DEVELOPING IDEAS AND MAKING THINGS HAPPEN				
Analysing and automating processes				
Use automated processes to increase efficiency (e.g. templates, master pages)	3	2d		1.5, 3.2
Represent simple processes as diagrams, showing:				
● how a task can be broken down into smaller ones	6	2b, 2d	7.6	6.2, 6.4, 6.5
● the sequence of operations, and any conditions or decisions that affect it	6	2b, 2d	7.6	6.2, 6.4, 6.5

(continued)

Framework	QCA SOW	NC POS	DfES Units	ICT Matters Unit
• the initial information needed (e.g. room temperature, price of items)	6	2b, 2d	7.6	6.2, 6.4, 6.5
Models and modelling				
Use software to investigate and amend a simple model by:				
• formatting and labelling data appropriately (e.g. formatting cells to display currency)	4	2c	7.4	4.1, 4.2, 4.3, 4.5
• entering rules or formulae and checking their appropriateness and accurate working	4	1c, 2c, 4a	7.4	4.1, 4.2, 4.3, 4.4, 4.5
• explaining the rules governing a model	4	2c	7.4	4.2, 4.3, 4.5
• predicting the effects of changing variables or rules	4	2c	7.4	4.4, 4.5
Test whether a simple model operates satisfactorily	4	4a	7.4	4.2, 4.3, 4.4, 4.5
Control and monitoring				
Implement a system to carry out a simple control task, including some that involve sensed physical data, by:				
• compiling sets of instructions, identifying those which can be grouped to form procedures or loops	6	2d	7.6	6.1, 6.3
• testing and refining the instructions	6	2d, 4a	7.6	6.3
EXCHANGING AND SHARING INFORMATION				
Fitness for purpose				
Recognise common forms and conventions used in communications and how these address audience needs (e.g. columns of text in newspapers, graphics and enlarged print in posters, hyperlinks on websites)	2,3	3a	7.3	3.6
Apply understanding of common forms and conventions to own ICT work	3	3a,3b	7.3	3.2, 3.6
Use given criteria to evaluate the effectiveness of own and others' publications and presentations	3	3a,3b,4a,4c	7.1, 7.3	1.5, 1.6, 3.2
Refining and presenting information				
Plan and design the presentation of information in digital media, taking account of the purpose of the presentation and intended audience	1, 3	3a, 3b	7.1, 7.3	1.1, 1.2, 1.3, 1.4, 1.5, 1.6, 3.2, 3.3, 3.6
Use ICT to draft and refine a presentation, including:				
• capturing still and moving images and sound (e.g. using a scanner, digital camera, microphone)	1, 3	3b	7.1, 7.3	1.2, 1.4, 3.3, 3.4, 3.5, 5.2
• re-organising, developing and combining information, including text, images and sound, using simple editing functions of common applications	1, 3, 4, 5	3b, 4a	7.1, 7.3	1.1, 1.2, 1.3, 1.4, 1.5, 3.1, 3.2, 3.3, 3.4, 3.5, 3.6
• importing and exporting data and information in appropriate formats	1, 3, 4, 5	3b, 3c	7.3	3.1, 3.2, 3.3, 3.4, 3.5, 3.6, 4.5, 5.1, 5.6
Communicating				
Use email securely and efficiently for short messages and supporting material		3c		See note on page 8
Know how to protect personal details and why this is important		4d	7.1	M1 PL, See note on page 7

Module 1
Creating a presentation

Where this module fits in	Prior learning
This module builds on: Work done in KS2 POS, particularly the 'Exchanging and sharing information' section.	To make good progress, pupils starting this module need to be able to: 1 Log onto the school network 2 Load and save work in a shared area, using the file naming conventions of the school 3 Edit, insert, delete, move, copy and paste text and pictures 4 Design a presentation: create slides, enter text and pictures
The main concept of this module is: That information can be communicated to an audience by means of a presentation which needs to address the needs of the audience and the purpose for which it is being given.	
This module leads on to: Other modules that require pupils to present their work, in particular Module 3 'Making a leaflet'.	Revision of these areas as in Module 1 Prior learning.

Subject knowledge needed by teachers

To teach this module you will need to know how to:	Information on this aspect can be found in:
Load and save work in a shared area	Pupil Book pages 1, 24
Use presentation software and create effective presentations	Pupil Book pages 24–31, Resource 1.6 Content checklist
Access sound and images from the network	Pupil Book pages 28, 30–31
Capture images using a digital camera	Pupil Book pages 30, 63, Resource 3.4 Acquiring images
Scan images using a scanner	Pupil Book page 29, Resource 3.4 Acquiring images
Add images to presentations and perform simple editing functions such as cropping, brightness and contrast	Pupil Book pages 28–30
Record and manipulate sounds using sound recording software	Pupil Book page 31
Add sounds to presentations	Pupil Book pages 30–31
Explain the differences between vector-based and bitmapped images	Pupil Book page 8, Resource 3.3 Vector logos

Level indicators
At the end of this module

Pupils working at Level 3 will:	Pupils working at Level 4 will:	Pupils working at Level 5 will:
• Find and use appropriate information for their presentations • Create and amend their presentations • Exchange ideas about their presentations with others	• Combine several different forms of information (e.g. insert images, sounds and words in their presentation) • Modify the raw information in their presentation, e.g. cropping an image • Refine the quality of their presentation showing an awareness of the needs of the audience	• Use a combination of tools in creating their presentation e.g. sound recording and editing s/w • Check the accuracy of information used • Structure and refine the information in their presentation and present it in different forms and styles for different purposes and audiences • Reflect critically on their presentation in order to make improvements to subsequent work

Overview of module content and how it fits with the DfES sample teaching units			
Module in Pupil Book	Matches DfES lesson (in terms of content and and teaching objectives covered)	Outline of content	Progress on Module Task
Module 1 Prior learning PB pages 1–3			
1.1 Putting in the content PB pages 4–6 TB pages 15–17	Lesson 7.1.1	Introduction to presentations. How to decide what content to include in a presentation. Introduction to concepts of purpose and audience.	Create content and insert it in presentation software. Order the contest using slide sorter.
1.2 Using images PB pages 7–10 TB pages 18–21	Lesson 7.1.2	Purposes of images in presentations. How to decide what images to use. Capturing images using a digital camera or a scanner. Adding images to presentation and editing them. Copyright.	Capture images and add them to presentation and edit if required. Comment on choices made.
1.3 Using fonts and colours PB pages 11–13 TB pages 22–24	Lesson 7.1.3	How fonts and colour can affect the quality and meaning of a presentation. How to alter fonts and colour in a presentation.	Modify the fonts and colour in the presentation and say why.
1.4 Using sounds PB pages 14–16 TB pages 25–27	Lesson 7.1.4	Purposes of sounds in presentations. How to decide what sounds to use. Capturing sounds using sound recorder. Adding sounds to presentation and editing them.	Add sounds to presentation and edit if required. Comment on choices made.
1.5 Changing the style of a presentation PB pages 17–19 TB pages 28–30	Lesson 7.1.5	Differences in conventions for presentations to adults and non-adults. How to apply consistency of style to a presentation.	Amend style of presentation for an adult audience.
1.6 Changing the content for a different audience PB pages 20–22 TB pages 31–33	Lesson 7.1.6	How similar content can vary for different audiences. How to evaluate a presentation against a set of given criteria, related to the audience.	Amend content of presentation for adult audience. Evaluate each others' presentations using given criteria.
Module 1 Assignment PB page 23 TB page 34	All of 7.1	Assignment covering the same learning objectives as those covered in Module lessons, but in the context of a visit to an outdoor pursuit centre. Scope for pupils to perform at Levels 3, 4 and 5.	

Cross curricular opportunities	
Subject	Programme of study section
English 3 (writing)	1h (using different font styles) 5c (presenting information)
Design and Technology Geography	1h (presenting designs using ICT) 1f (communicate/present data) 6g (presenting information about settlements)
MFL	2j (creating and amending texts using ICT) 5d (producing and responding to ICT texts)
Art RE	2a (using images for a purpose) Sharing ideas using ICT

Unit 1.1
Putting in the content

In this unit pupils learn that information can be communicated to an audience by means of a presentation. They will start to create their own presentation by inserting and organising some content using presentation software.

Supports DfES sample teaching unit 7.1.1

ICT Framework Objectives

EXCHANGING AND SHARING INFORMATION

Refining and presenting information

- Plan and design the presentation of information in digital media, taking account of the purpose of the presentation and intended audience.
- Use ICT to draft and refine a presentation, including re-organising, using the simple editing functions of common applications.

Key vocabulary

audience, bullet point, draft, image, log on, network, plan, presentation software, purpose, shared area

Resources

Pupil Book: Module 1 Unit 1, pages 4–6
Resource 1.1 My pets
Resource 1.1 School information 1 (poor version)
Resource 1.1 School information 2 (good version)
PowerPoint loaded onto display board in Outline mode
Computers with sound cards and headphones
Large screen display for demonstrations and pupil presentations

Suggested lesson plan

Starter
The suggested Starters introduce pupils to the different situations in which presentations are given. They consider content, audience and style of presentation. Class discussions allow them to air their thoughts and obtain feedback from the class.

Main part
Task 1 draws together responses from the class to a prepared presentation. In Task 2 they think about the content of two presentations – one good and one bad, and decide which was more successful in communicating the message. Some pupils will work at a higher level of critical comment by completing Task 3. The concepts of purpose and audience are introduced on page 5 of the Pupil Book.

The Module Task allows pupils to create their own presentation. Pupils work in pairs to put together a presentation of six slides about each of them.

Plenary
Select one or two pupils to show their presentations on the large display. Encourage others to contribute and draw out the key features of what they have learned. Help pupils to evaluate the presentations in terms of whether the content is suitable for the purpose and audience by asking questions based on those on page 5 of the Pupil Book.

Differentiation
Task 3 may be used as a 'stretch' activity for more able pupils to consider how they might change their presentation for a different audience.

Suggested starters

1   Ask pupils to name three different situations in which they experience people presenting information to them in different ways – suggestions could include assembly, theatre groups and on-display monitors. Ask them to describe how and why the methods of presentation need to be different.

2   Provide pupils with a series of words that could be used for the same item, for example an item of clothing. The idea is to make them realise that things are described in different ways for different reasons and audiences.

3   Allow not more than five minutes for pupils to list all of the ways that information is presented to them during an average day from the time of getting out of bed. Their list should include all formats of information. Compile the 'class list' of information sources and the range of equipment that is used to convey the information.

Notes on Tasks

Task 1 (Green)

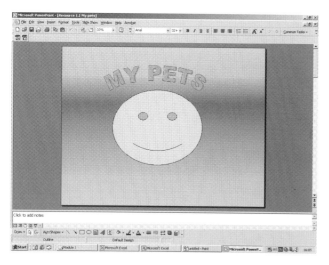

Pupils watch the presentation on **Resource 1.1 My pets** for this task. They should make notes about the presentation and feed back to the rest of the class. This presentation was created by an 11-year-old and could form the basis for a discussion about many of the issues which will be covered in this module, such as consistency, appropriate use of images, fonts, etc.

Task 2 (Green)

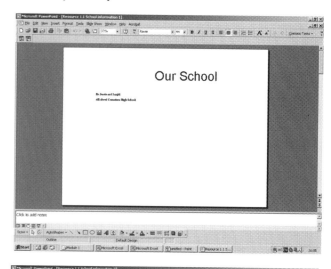

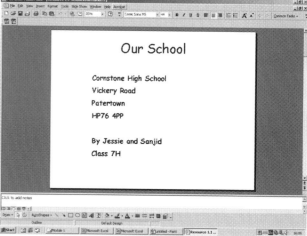

Pupils watch the presentations in **Resource 1.1 School information 1** and **Resource 1.1 School information 2** and evaluate their success in communicating their messages.

Task 3 (Red)

Although all pupils could manage this task, it could be used as a differentiated activity with pupils working towards the higher levels. Pupils may discuss this as a group, in pairs or write down personal opinions.

Module Task

You may need to demonstrate how to enter slide headings and organise them using slide view. You could get pupils to do the first part of the Module Task and feed suggestions for headings to you to be used in your demonstration. This would then form a class example which pupils can use as a guide. However, it is important to stress that this is their presentation and they can change some of the headings and the order if they want to. Pupils will need to print off their presentation or take it home electronically, if they are to complete Task 4 as homework.

Task 4 (Green)

Pupils should be encouraged to keep all drafts of work and to view critical annotation as a positive activity. They may need help at the beginning of the course with the filenaming of different drafts.

Homework suggestion

Pupils complete Task 4. They could collect images to add to their presentations.
For Unit 1.2 you may need to provide sources of images, e.g. magazines/files.

Suggested extension activity

As an additional activity pupils could:

1 Look at the bullet points on one of their slides, for example they might have a slide on hobbies including football, karate and watching TV.
2 Copy each bullet point onto a new slide so that it becomes a new heading.
3 Add in additional information under the new heading. For example under the heading of 'Football' they could add details about their favourite team, where they play, what position they play.
4 Save their latest version of the presentation.

Level guide

Level 5

Pupils working at Level 5 and above will provide headings that are presented in a logical order and relate to the information provided on the slide. They will justify and make changes to improve their presentation.

Level 4

Pupils working at Level 4 will use headings that inform the viewer as to the content of each slides. They will be able to identify items that they would change and provide realistic reasons for the change.

Level 3

Pupils working at Levels 3 and below will produce slides where the headings are vague and/or do not form a logical sequence. The information on the slides will be poor and have no direction.

Unit 1.2
Using images

In this unit pupils will learn how images can be used to give information or add interest to a presentation. They format images correctly and add them into their presentation through the use of a scanner or digital camera.

Supports DfES sample teaching unit 7.1.2

ICT Framework Objectives

EXCHANGING AND SHARING INFORMATION

Refining and presenting information

- Plan and design the presentation of information in digital media, taking account of the purpose of the presentation and intended audience.
- Use ICT to draft and refine a presentation, including:
  - capturing still and moving images (e.g. using a scanner, digital camera)
  - combining text and images, using the simple editing functions of common applications.

Key vocabulary

bitmapped graphic, copyright, digital camera, fitness for purpose, scanner, vector graphic

Suggested lesson plan

Starter
Pupils make themselves familiar with all the different types of image from cartoons, illustrations, photographs, line drawings, paintings and electronic formats. They discuss the power of images and the ways in which they can replace words and form an international language.

Main part
The unit involves whole class teaching on how different images are used for different purposes. It includes demonstrations of the following: using a scanner; using a digital camera; selecting and inserting clip art; using simple editing techniques from the picture toolbar such as cropping, brightness and contrast.

Resources

Pupil Book: Module 1 Unit 2, pages 7–10

Resource 1.2 What's it for?

Resource 1.2 Images

Resource 1.2 Formats

Resource 1.2 School information 3 (poor version)

Resource 1.2 School information 4 (good version)

Presentation software

Image Bank

Scanner

Digital camera

Selection of images from magazines/files including photographs, illustrations, cartoons, line drawings

Task 2 gives practice on the difference between vector and bitmapped images, and the Module Task focuses on choosing images that are fit for purpose. More able pupils can tackle Task 4.

Plenary
Select one or two pupils to show their presentations on the large display. Encourage other pupils to contribute and draw out the key features of what they have learned. Help pupils to evaluate their own use of images against what they have learned in Task 3.

Differentiation
Most pupils will be able to acquire images and manipulate them but the more able pupils will be able to consider format types and use them effectively in their presentation.

Suggested starters

1 Whole class activity. Discuss with the whole class the reason why images can be more useful than words, for example in foreign countries where symbols can clearly give directions. Make a list of the ways in which images can replace words.

2 Pupils work in pairs. Give each pair a book, film or song title. Tell one of the pair to draw the title for the other to guess, then vice versa. Discuss what the problems were in trying to use images to depict the item.

3 Whole class activity. Compile a list of the different types of images that are used with the whole class. The list should contain items such as cartoons, illustration, photographs, line drawings, paintings, electronic formats. If you have collected a range of examples, these could be distributed among the pupils. Ask pupils to discuss in pairs the problems and limitations of using different types of images, for example a line drawing of a house for sale may not give the correct impression of the real property. If appropriate to pupils' ability, discuss copyright.

Notes on Tasks

Task 1 (Green)

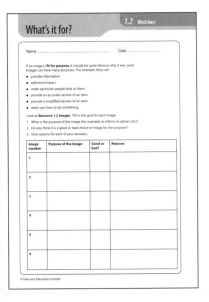

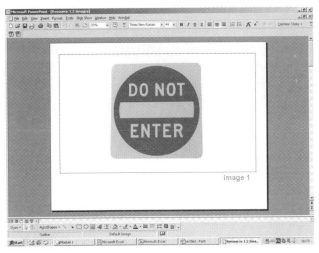

After looking at **Resource 1.2 Images**, pupils complete a table on the worksheet, **Resource 1.2 What's it for?** This makes them consider why and how the images are used. They are also asked to give a purpose for having the images within a specified type of document. Compile a class list of their results on a whiteboard/flip chart to see whether there was general agreement as to why the images might be used and the type of item they might be used in.

Task 2 (Green)

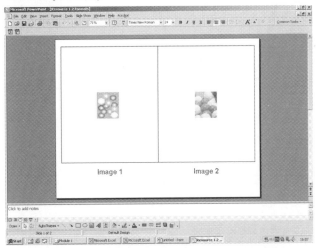

Pupils look at and work with **Resource 1.2 Formats**. They will need to be in **outline view** in order to be able to manipulate the images. The purpose of the task is to illustrate the differences in file format.

Task 3 (Green)

Pupils look at **Resource 1.2 School information 3** and **Resource 1.2 School information 4**. A simple evaluation task to make the pupils look at two PowerPoint presentations, one of which (**Resource 1.2 School information 3**) has images that have been placed inaccurately, the other (**Resource 1.2 School information 4**) has images more carefully placed.

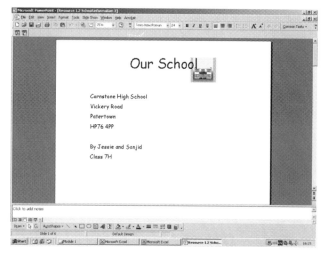

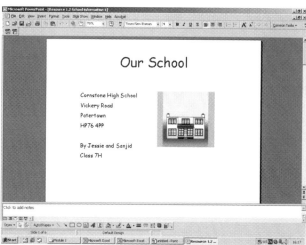

Module Task

Before starting on this task it will probably be necessary to give a demonstration of how to use the equipment that is available for pupils to capture their images. It will be necessary to show how to:

- insert a piece of clip art (see page 28 of the Pupil Book)
- download an image from the Internet (see page 28 of Pupil Book)
- obtain an image using a digital camera (see page 30 of Pupil Book)

- scan in a hand-drawn image, magazine clip (copyright permitting) or photograph (see page 29 of Pupil Book).

Task 4 (Red)

The purpose of this task is to identify how far students are able to manipulate images to fit with different spaces, content, etc. The image chosen should be seen as 'decoration' of the slides. Most pupils will be able to complete some of this task but some pupils will be able to manipulate images with a high level of skill.

Task 5 (Green)

Pupils make decisions about the impact that the images have had upon their presentations and annotate where they would like to make improvements.

They are asked to collect a range of printed items that appeal to them because of colour, layout, image and presentation. You may need to provide additional items for the pupils to work with in Unit 1.3.

Homework suggestion

Pupils could do Task 5, collecting a range of printed items that have images, text and colour.

Suggested extension activity

As an additional activity pupils could:

1 Open a presentation program such as MS PowerPoint.

2 Set up a new blank presentation.

3 Use a range of the shape tools to create a vector graphic that they could use to represent a bullet point on one of their slides, for example if one of their hobbies is rugby, they could create a rugby ball from the circle and ellipse tools.

4 Get help with creating vector graphics on page 30 of the Pupil Book.

5 Insert the image onto the correct slide in the other presentation created for this unit.

6 Save their presentation.

Level guide

Level 5

Pupils working at Level 5 and above will be able to manipulate images to create effects that they want. They will be able to import images from a range of sources and to have the ability to discriminate between the format types for effective use in their presentation.

Level 4

Pupils working at Level 4 will acquire images from both a scanner and camera. They will be able to manipulate images by enlarging, stretching and cropping. They will be able to discuss the different format of images and the effects of saving them in different formats.

Level 3

Pupils working at Levels 3 and below will insert images such as clip art. They will not consider where they are placed and may not attempt to manipulate them to improve the appearance of the slide.

Unit 1.3

Using fonts and colours

Supports DfES sample teaching unit 7.1.3

ICT Framework Objectives

EXCHANGING AND SHARING INFORMATION

Refining and presenting information

- *Plan and design the presentation of information in digital media, taking account of the purpose of the presentation and intended audience.*
- *Use ICT to draft and refine a presentation by changing the format of the text, using the simple editing functions of common applications.*

Key vocabulary

attribute, case/upper case/lower case, document, bold, font, font size, format, heading, hyperlink, italic, multimedia, onscreen, style, underline, viewing, subheading

Suggested lesson plan

Starter

Pupils are given practise in categorising colours and the impact they have on consumers. They are also given the opportunity to examine the difference in the impact of a word when different fonts are used.

Main part

Task 1 reviews styles and sizes of fonts and Task 2 reinforces learning on different font attributes. Task 3 allows more able pupils to consider the type of font they would use in a series of different contexts. Combined use of colours and text are used in Task 4 and in the Module Task pupils edit their presentation to maximise the effect of the font attributes and colour. They focus on why they are making the changes and their reason for them.

Plenary

Pupils discuss in pairs and write down guidelines about use of colours and fonts

Resources

Pupil Book: Module 1 Unit 3, pages 11–13

Resource 1.3 Fonts

Resource 1.3 Order

Resource 1.3 Colours

Resource 1.3 Font puzzles

Presentation software

A range of printed items that use colour, images and layout, e.g. advertisements, leaflets

in presentations. Draw these together in class discussion to check understanding.

Differentiation

Most pupils will discriminate between font attributes and make reasonable suggestions for which ones to use. More able pupils will be able to go on and maximise the use of the software tools to enhance the way the colour can be used. They may also be more consistent and systematic in the way they apply their techniques.

Suggested starters

1   Whole class activity. In a box place the wrappers of three different everyday items, e.g. chocolate bar wrapper, tube of toothpaste, shampoo bottle. Ask a pupil to come out and look into the box. They have to write on the flipchart/board the colours that are used on the item. The outcome should start to help pupils to categorise colours and the impact that they have on us.

2 Pupils split into groups of four/five. Each group is given some paint colour sample strips. They are asked to cut up the strips to create combination colour schemes that they think could be used in different types of presentations, e.g. they could choose pinks/creams for presenting a new ice cream, they could use blues and dark greens for a presentation about underwater holidays.

3 Whole class activity. Provide pupils with the same word reproduced in different fonts. The word needs to be something that creates a visual image, for example, the word 'Circus'. The variations of the word should be produced in the wrong fonts and colours, only one being a typical one for the word. Ask the pupils to vote on the font and colours that they think provide the correct combination.

Notes on Tasks

Task 1 (Green)

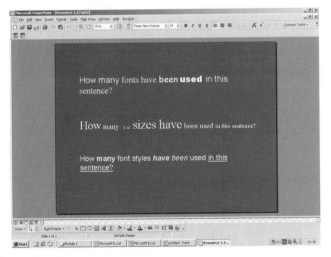

Pupils work in pairs to look at **Resource 1.3 Fonts**, that asks them about the fonts used in the slide show. The purpose of the task is to develop an awareness of some common font attributes. Pupils should make a list of their answers. Have a class discussion to agree the answers.

Task 2 (Green)

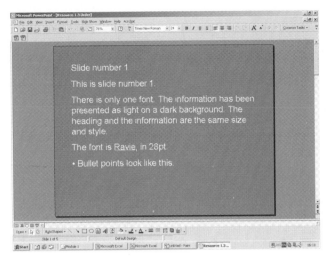

Pupils look at **Resource 1.3 Order**. The purpose of this task is to make pupils start to discriminate between the readability and visual impact of various font and colour combinations. They are asked to sort the slides into the order that appeals to them the most with the first slide being the best. Pupils add notes to the file and print it in note form. Pupils will need to be able to use **Outline** and **Note View**.

Ask them to look at the Skills help on pages 24–31 of the Pupil Book if necessary.

Task 3 (Red)

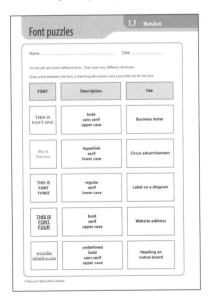

Pupils working at the higher levels carry out an exercise based upon font attributes. They look at the worksheet **Resource 1.3 Font puzzles**, which prompts them to link each font with a description and a possible use for the font.

Task 4 (Green)

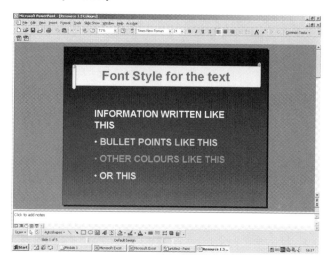

This task could be done as a whole class activity. All pupils look at **Resource 1.3 Colours**. This task can be used as the basis for a class discussion about the use of the different colour schemes to capture an effect or atmosphere. Get pupils to help you match the best slides for each purpose and then describe how the remaining slide could be used. The additional slide that does not have an allocated scenario could potentially be used to introduce a film or book.

Module Task

The purpose of the Module Task is to allow pupils the opportunity to improve their presentations by identifying fonts that are suitable for the different slides. They are asked to review their use of fonts and to make changes as necessary. Pupils annotate a printout of their presentation to indicate where and why they have made alterations.

Task 5 (Green)

The purpose of this task is to develop a broader understanding of how different font styles and colours can affect us. Pupils record their feelings about five multimedia advertisements stating what attributes attracted them. They are asked to compare how these attributes could work in print media.

Homework Suggestion

Pupils could do Task 5 at home.

Suggested extension activity

As an additional activity for more able pupils, pupils could:

1 Design their own letters for a font set on some squared paper.
They should start with the letters in their name and create both the upper and lower case versions.

2 They then list the attributes that the font has and suggest suitable scenarios for its use.

Level guide

Level 5

Pupils working at Level 5 and above will be able to discriminate between the font attributes to make a reasoned and appropriate selection for use in their presentation. They will be able to maximise the use of the software tools to enhance the way the colour can be used.

Level 4

Pupils working at Level 4 will discriminate between font attributes and make reasonable suggestions for which ones to use. They will not be consistent in the way they apply the use of software tools and techniques to maximise the use of colour schemes.

Level 3

Pupils working at Levels 3 and below will be able to change font attributes but will not be discerning in their choice of fonts or colours.

Unit 1.4
Using sounds

In this unit pupils will learn how to add appropriate sounds to their presentation.

Supports DfES sample teaching unit 7.1.4

ICT Framework Objectives

EXCHANGING AND SHARING INFORMATION

Refining and presenting information

● Plan and design the presentation of information in digital media, taking account of the purpose of the presentation and intended audience.

● Use ICT to draft and refine a presentation, including:
  – capturing sound
  – re-organising, developing and combining information, including text, images and sound, using the simple editing functions of common applications.

Key vocabulary

animate, microphone, sound, speaker, voice-over

Suggested lesson plan

Starter

The suggested Starters provide a platform for pupils to consider how sounds can replace words and the idea of recognisable catch-phrases associated with famous characters. They are given the opportunity to come up with the sound effects for the introduction to a horror movie.

Main part

Task 1 involves identifying some sounds and discussing associated feelings and storylines. After whole class teaching/demonstration on finding sound files, inserting them into presentation software and creating a voice-over, you can ask the pupils to carry out Task 2 and then the Module Task. They will gain experience of selecting sounds and inserting them into their own presentations.

Pupils can then carry out Task 4 and evaluate each other's presentations in pairs. Less able pupils may need guidance on selecting appropriate sounds. More able pupils can be asked to tackle Task 3.

Resources

Pupil Book: Module 1 Unit 4, pages 14–16
Resource 1.4 Sounds
Resource 1.4 Sounds like what?
Resource 1.4 Sound sense
Resource 1.4 TV sound log
Computers with sound cards installed, speakers and headphones
Microphones and sound recording equipment
Presentation software
Sound files from CD ROM Soundbank, clip art or the Internet
Internet access

Plenary

Draw together pupils' comments from Task 4 into a class discussion about the main points learnt in this lesson.

Differentiation

Most pupils will be able to add sound files from a range of sources into their presentations. More able pupils will be able to adjust the settings for the timing of the sound and have some working automatically and some when activated by the user. A further challenge will come in distinguishing the different needs of voice-over from sound effect and how they can both be used in different settings.

Suggested starters

1   Whole class activity. Base this upon sound effects and how they can be used to replace words. Ask for examples of the sounds that they would expect to hear in an introduction to:

● a murder/mystery play

● a children's TV programme

● a story about life at sea.

2 Whole class activity. Pupils think of catch-phrases of famous cartoon characters, for example 'Bugs Bunny', and describe them to a partner. Partner has to guess what the character is. The purpose is to try and get pupils to appreciate the different types of sound used to portray different types of characters.

3 Whole class activity. Pupils are given five minutes to come up with their own version of sound effects for an introduction to a horror movie. Write a list of words on the board from which the pupils create their own story line, for example scream, howl, slammed door, breaking glass. Select pairs of pupils as time permits to re-enact their introductions.

Notes on Tasks

In order to hear the sound files embedded in the resources, pupils will need to be in **Slide Show** mode.

Task 1 (Green)

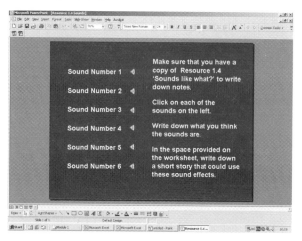

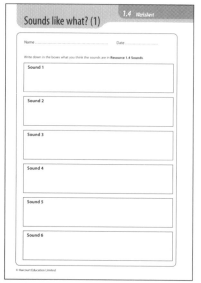

Pupils work in pairs. They open **Resource 1.4 Sounds** and follow the onscreen instructions. The purpose of the task is to make the pupils consider how combinations of sounds can be used to make us feel things or tell a story. They use the worksheet, **Resource 1.4 Sounds like what?** to complete a storyline based upon the sounds that they hear. They discuss their storyline and then feedback to the rest of the group.

Task 2 (Green)

Pupils make onscreen notes about the sounds that they could potentially add to their presentation. They will be adding these to the notes made in the last unit, unless they are advised to overwrite these. They do not need to print out the presentation as long as they remember to save it with the notes in place. Having spent time thinking about what they *could* add, they then are asked to work out what they *should* add. They make notes about the type of sound and how it should be used. Pupils working at the lower levels will need assistance in determining where sounds should be added.

Task 3 (Red)

Pupils working at the higher levels are asked to set up their presentation to run as an automated presentation. They have to create some voice-over files to add in. These need to be set to run automatically when the slide opens and finish before the next one starts. Pupils might need assistance in setting the timing to ensure that the information can be read and the sound files heard before one slide moves onto the next.

For help with sound recording and automating a presentation refer pupils to the Skills help on page 31 of the Pupil Book.

Module Task

Before pupils can carry out the Module Task you may need to demonstrate how to download sounds and how to use the sound recorder. Pupils add their selected sounds (from Task 2) into their presentation. Some pupils might be downloading files from the Internet. They will need to know where to save them in the shared area to be able to access them when working on their presentation.

Task 4 (Green)

Pupils work in pairs and evaluate each other's work. They complete the worksheet, **Resource 1.4 Sound sense** that contains a list of questions about the way they have used sound in their presentation. This task could be used as a plenary, drawing individuals' comments together in a whole class discussion.

Task 5 (Green)

Pupils are asked to carry out an exercise between the end of this lesson and the next one. They are to use the worksheet, **Resource 1.4 TV sound log** to record the differences in the way that the TV presenters appear at the different time slots and to describe the way that they think this has been done to attract an audience that is watching at the time.

Homework suggestion

Pupils could do Task 5 as homework.

Suggested extension activity

As an additional activity pupils could:

1   Select one of the slides that they have created within their presentation.
2   Add in sound files for each of the items on the slide, but 'hide' the speaker icon.
3   Set the multimedia animation tool to happen on mouse over.
4   Enjoy watching a partner jump when 'invisible' noises come out of their presentation!

Level guide

Level 5
Pupils working at Level 5 and above will be able to discriminate between sound files they select and those that they create themselves. They will be able to set them up to run automatically with the correct time setting. They will be able to distinguish the different needs of voice-over from sound effect and how they can both be used in different settings.

Level 4
Pupils working at Level 4 will be able to add sound files from a range of sources into their presentations. They will be able to adjust the settings for the timing of the sound and have some working automatically and some when activated by the user. They may not always select the correct type of sound file, e.g. sound effect instead of voice.

Level 3
Pupils working at Levels 3 and below will be able to add sound files into their presentation. They may not discriminate between the types of sounds and they will not always be appropriate to the slide being displayed.

Unit 1.5
Changing the style of a presentation

In this unit pupils learn how to alter their presentation for different audiences. They also find out how to set up a presentation so that each slide has the same appearance.

Supports DfES sample teaching unit 7.1.5

ICT Framework Objectives

EXCHANGING AND SHARING INFORMATION

Fitness for purpose
- *Use given criteria to evaluate the effectiveness of own and others' presentations.*

Refining and presenting information
- *Plan and design the presentation of information in digital media, taking account of the purpose of the presentation and intended audience.*
- *Use ICT to refine a presentation by re-organising information, including text, images and sound, using the simple editing functions of common applications.*

Suggested lesson plan

Starter
The suggested Starters introduce pupils to the different situations in which presentations are given. They consider audience and venue. Class discussions allow pupils to air their thoughts and obtain feedback from the class.

Main part
Task 1 provides a performance checklist for the pupils to use as reference in future work. They can then move on to Task 2 to practise changing backgrounds in their presentations. The Module Task challenges pupils to change their presentation to suit a different audience in a particular venue. As part of the Module Task, pupils carry out an evaluation of their own presentation and that of a partner.

DEVELOPING IDEAS AND MAKING THINGS HAPPEN

Analysing and automating processes
- *Use automated processes to increase efficiency (e.g. templates, master pages).*

Key vocabulary
annotate, criterion, evaluate, judge, template

Resources
Pupil Book: Module 1 Unit 5, pages 17–19
Resource 1.5 Performance checklist
Presentation software

In Task 4 pupils annotate their work to show how they have altered their presentation to match the new audience, and they make suggestions for further improvement.

Plenary
Draw together the main points arising out of the paired evaluations in the Module Task. Ask pupils which styles they prefer and why. Ask if they would like to make any changes to their original presentation in the light of what they have learnt about consistency of style.

Differentiation
More able pupils will be able to make changes to their presentation efficiently using the automated features of the software. Less able pupils may need help with this.

Suggested starters

1   Whole class activity. Ask pupils to give three words to describe different venues, for example an assembly hall, a theatre, a classroom. Compile a list that brings out different features of the three, for example light, dark, quiet. The purpose will be to discuss the different requirements of a presentation in these different venues.

2   Whole class activity. Provide pupils with a series of words on cards that they have to put together to make a set of criteria for the development of a presentation. The words should allow them to make up different types of venue for presentations, for example hall, classroom, office, theatre, that could be linked with dark, bright, dimly lit, daylight, artificial lighting, etc. The purpose is to make them think about the different venues and the constraints that these impose upon a presentation.

3   Whole class activity. On a flipchart compile a list of all the adjectives that pupils can come up with to describe a target audience. This could be related to something that is happening in the school, for example an open evening or a specific group of people such as a nursery class. The purpose is to discuss how the nature of the audience determines what a presentation needs to offer.

Notes on Tasks

Task 1 (Green)

In this task pupils simply look at the list of questions on the worksheet, **Resource 1.5 Performance checklist** and consider what sort of issues each one raises. For example, the question 'Will it be dark or light?' might prompt them to think about issues such as font colour/size and background colours, whilst 'How old are they?' might make them think about the balance of words to images on a slide.

Task 2 (Green)

Pupils browse and select from the backgrounds that are available to them through the software. They are asked to consider the effect of a background for different types of audience.

Note: By this stage there could be a wide variety of different presentations. For example, more able pupils may have added voice-overs and automated their presentations. Others may have added additional slides with more detail on certain aspects. If possible pupils should amend what they already have, rather than starting afresh for the new audience. You may need to group pupils together according to how far they have got with enhancing/automating their presentations.

Module Task

Pupils create their own performance checklist by answering the questions on the worksheet, **Resource 1.5 Performance checklist** to create an edited version of their presentation. This could be introduced through a reminder of the type of things they should be considering. Stress that they are looking at the style not the content in this task. They have to alter the presentation to make it consistent in appearance and be suitable for viewing by an audience of teachers and pupils in an assembly hall. Pupils save their presentation with a new file name that should reflect the fact that this is a new presentation for a different audience. They alter their presentation and then present it to a partner. They will then review their partner's presentation. Pupils should be able to justify the decisions they have made. More able pupils could be asked what changes they might make if the presentation was to be shown on a continuous loop in a crowded hall at an open day.

Task 3 (Red)

Pupils working at the higher levels will make use of the **Slide Master** to create a template for their presentation.

Task 4 (Green)

Pupils print out their presentation and annotate it to show where they have made alterations and where they would like to make improvements. They then send their presentation to MS Word in **Outline View** to become a storyboard. They use this storyboard to plan how to change the **content** of the presentation for a group of teachers and pupils.

Homework suggestion

Pupils do part 3 of Task 4: using the storyboard to plan how to change the content. They will either need to take the storyboard home electronically, or print it off to work on it at home.

Suggested extension activity

As an additional activity pupils could:

1   Open their presentation in **Outline View**.
2   Make **Speaker's Notes** about each of the slides that would help them to present without having to read the slide.
    The notes should add to the information and not repeat it.
3   Rehearse their delivery of the presentation so they know when to click to move between the slides, or set up a transition effect to move between the slides.
4   Save the latest version of their presentation.

Level guide

Level 5

Pupils working at Level 5 and above will create a **Slide Master** template for use in their presentation. They will enhance their presentation by creating a suitable background that has a balance between the chosen background and the fonts used. They will be able to discriminate between the use of a wide range of fonts and those suitable to provide information effectively. They will make sound judgements about the criteria for developing a presentation and in their evaluations.

Level 4

Pupils working at Level 4 will create a consistent presentation that has a suitable background applied to each slide. Their choice of fonts will be appropriate to the subject and they will demonstrate the ability to make judgements about the work of others. They will be able to work within the limits of the criteria.

Level 3

Pupils working at Levels 3 and below will produce slides where backgrounds do not always enhance the appearance of the slide. They will be able to work with a limited range of fonts but the choice of fonts will not add to the presentation. They will have difficulty in evaluating their presentation against the set criteria.

Unit 1.6
Changing the content for a different audience

In this unit pupils will learn how to alter the content of a presentation for a different audience, and how to evaluate a presentation.

Supports DfES sample teaching unit 7.1.6

ICT Framework Objectives

EXCHANGING AND SHARING INFORMATION

Fitness for purpose
● *Use given criteria to evaluate the effectiveness of own and others' presentations.*

Refining and presenting information
● *Plan and design the presentation of information in digital media, taking account of the purpose of the presentation and intended audience.*

Key vocabulary
annotate, criteria, effective, feature

Resources
Pupil Book: Module 1 Unit 6, pages 20–22
Resource 1.6 Content checklist
Resource 1.6 Evaluation list
Resource 1.6 Transitions
Presentation software

Suggested lesson plan

Starter
The Starters make pupils consider words/vocabulary and how meaning can be supported by visual material. They also consider how different audiences relate differently to presentations.

Main part
Task 1 allows pupils to review their presentations and feed back the results of their discussions on changing content for a teacher-and-pupil audience. The Module Task allows pupils to carry out the changes they recommended in Unit 1.5. More able pupils can refine their presentations by carrying out Task 2. The Module Task is drawn to a conclusion in Task 3 where pupils evaluate the presentations from the class.

Plenary
A class discussion on the evaluation points for the Module Task established in Task 3. Pupils look back at their original presentation aimed at their peer group and consider in what ways it would not be suitable for a wider or different audience.

Differentiation
Most pupils will be confident in amending their presentations to include an adult audience. More able pupils will be able to edit their presentations in terms of layout, content and vocabulary. Some will include further refinement by ensuring relevance and clarity of content.

Suggested starters

1   Whole class activity. Provide pupils with a list of long or complicated words that have simple alternatives, for example precipitation = rain. The purpose of the activity is to make the pupils develop an awareness of how important it is to use appropriate vocabulary in their presentation.

2   Whole class activity. Provide pupils with a series of words that have duplicate meanings, for example, 'Monitor'. Ask them what the word means and always contradict them by providing the alternative meaning. The purpose will be to show how, even when the words are spoken or written, it is sometimes important to have a visual support by means of an image.

3 Whole class activity. Save a series of web pages as images. Some should be appropriate to the class as an audience and some should not. Show them to the pupils in rapid succession and only for a short period of time. Ask them what they have seen. Discuss the different images and which ones they can recall, ask them why. The purpose of the activity will be to make them relate to the websites and how they remember the ones that were directed towards them as an audience.

Notes on Tasks

Task 1 (Green)

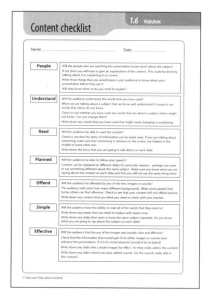

Pupils are asked to consider the content of their presentation against various criteria. The Helpsheet, **Resource 1.6 Content checklist** provides them with a framework for recording their judgements.
The evaluation should be done on the basis of the teacher-and-pupil audience, not the peer group audience.

Module Task
Pupils use the storyboard that they have created in Unit 1.5 plus the notes they made in Task 1 to help them to make changes to their teacher-and-pupil presentation.
They print out the latest version of their presentation and show it to a partner.

Task 2 (Red)

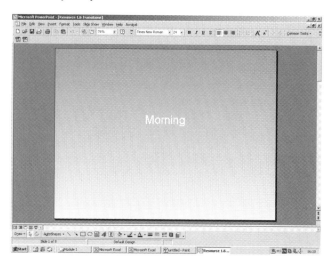

Pupils working to the higher levels are asked to use slide transitions and automated timing to enhance their presentations. You need to draw out from them why they have chosen a particular transition style, and under what circumstances an automated presentation is appropriate. **Resource 1.6 Transititions** can be used as an exemplar.

Task 3 (Green)

This task should be used as the basis for a class discussion about features that can be fairly evaluated in any presentation. Pupils draw up their own list of features and explain how they would make judgements. As a class they compile an evaluation list using the worksheet **Resource 1.6 Evaluation list** as the template file. They then carry out evaluations of at least two presentations that they have not seen before, using the list.

Once pupils have received feedback, they should print out their presentation and annotate it to show where they have made alterations and where they would like to make improvements.

Homework suggestion

Pupils could write a brief report that highlights what they have learnt throughout the module.

Suggested extension activity

As an additional activity pupils could:

1   Open the latest version of their presentation.
2   Record a new voice-over suitable for an adult audience.
3   If they have not already done so, they could automate their presentation using the new voice-over.

Level guide

Level 5

Pupils working at Level 5 and above will amend the content of their presentations to ensure relevance and clarity. They will make use of slide transitions to enhance their presentations and will ensure that the nature of the timing and transitions is effective rather than distracting.

Level 4

Pupils working at Level 4 will edit their presentations to match the new audience. They will make reasonable judgements about the layout of the contents and will look to change wording where it is poor or has no relevance to the new audience. Some will make use of transitions but will not apply them in a consistent way.

Level 3

Pupils working at Levels 3 and below will amend their presentations to try to match an adult audience. They will not check for accuracy and the presentation will have little relevance to the audience although it may run effectively.

Module 1
The Sejour Centre

Assignment

To complete Module 1 pupils are required to produce a presentation for an outdoor pursuits centre.

Resources

Pupil Book: Module 1, pages 1–31
Module 1 Assignment Evaluation form
PowerPoint or similar presentation software
Sound cards and headphones

National Curriculum Level indicators based upon pupil outcome

Level indicators At the end of this assignment		
Pupils working at Level 3 will: • Make use of the information supplied within their presentation • Make sensible use of the 6 slides • Amend their presentations to make it suitable for Year 6 pupils • Need help making changes for an adult audience • With prompting, talk about what they have done	Pupils working at Level 4 will: • Make use of the information supplied within their presentation and add to it with relevant information from different sources • Present the 6 slides in a logical order • Use language and images appropriate for a Year 6 pupil • Show their presentation to the rest of the group • Identify and make changes to content and layout to suit an adult audience	Pupils working at Level 5 will: • Make use of the information supplied through the use of a combination of tools; supplement these with their own materials and those from a range of different sources e.g. sound recording and editing • Check the accuracy of their presentation and the information used • Structure and refine the information for a Year 6 audience • Show their presentation to an appropriate audience, e.g. a group of Year 6 pupils • Confidently change words, layout and images to suit an adult audience • Reflect critically on their presentation in order to make improvements to subsequent work

Module 2
Using data and information sources

Overview

Where this module fits in	Prior learning
This module builds on: Work done in KS2 POS, particularly the 'Finding things out' section.	To make good progress, pupils starting this module need to be able to: 1 Access the Internet 2 Use URLs and connect to specific websites 3 Navigate websites to gain information 4 Appreciate different types of questions can be used to gain information
The main concept of this module is: That information can be gathered from a wide range of sources and care needs to be taken to make sure that information gathered is relevant to the task. The reliability of data needs to be questioned and methods of checking and authenticating sources must be identified.	
This module leads on to: Other units that require pupils to find information from a range of sources and ask relevant questions, particularly in Module 5 'Data handling'.	Revision of these areas is in Module 2 Prior learning.

Subject knowledge needed by teachers

To teach this module you will need to know how to:	Information on this aspect can be found in:
Load and save work in a shared area	Pupil Book pages 1, 24
Devise sensible samples/questions	Pupil Book pages 35–37, Resource 2.1 Cats, Resource 2.1 Holidays, Resource 2.1 Questions
Use the Internet to access information	Pupil Book pages 32, 38–42, 49
Make selective searches	Pupil Book pages 41, 43–44, Resource 2.3 Comparisons Resource 2.3 What it says, Resource 2.3 Words
Understand copyright restrictions	Pupil Book page 10

Level indicators
At the end of this module

Pupils working at Level 3 will:
- Find and use appropriate stored information following straightforward lines of enquiry
- Identify sources of appropriate stored information following straightforward lines of enquiry
- Work in a collaborative way with partners
- Exchange information with others

Pupils working at Level 4 will:
- Find relevant information that comes from a range of sources
- Create carefully phrased questions to gain specific information
- Interpret the results of their questioning and recognise that poor quality questions will provide unreliable results

Pupils working at Level 5 will:
- Make a reasoned decision as to which efficient sources of information to use for gaining specified information for a task
- Consider the qualitative and quantitative nature of information gained
- Phrase questions in such a way as to gather the information needed without gaining any unrelated information
- Check the accuracy of information used and present it in a form suitable for processing

Overview of module content and how it fits with the DfES sample teaching units			
Module in Pupil Book	Matches DfES lesson (in terms of content and and teaching objectives covered)	Outline of content	Progress on Module Task
Module 2 Prior learning PB pages 32–33			
2.1 Information for a purpose PB pages 34–37 TB pages 37–40	Lesson 7.2.1	Identifying the sources for and purposes of different types of information, identifying how to gather information that is meaningful by carefully phrasing questions, and questioning accuracy of information gathered.	Create questions, set up sample for questions, collect responses, and provide meaningful feedback.
2.2 Selecting sources and finding information PB pages 38–42 TB pages 41–43	Lesson 7.2.2	Finding efficient ways of finding information from websites or other sources. Using Internet search engines.	Retrieving information in the most efficient way from a website. Trying to minimise the web pages to be visited to gain specified information.
2.3 Assessing reliability of information PB pages 43–45 TB pages 44–46	Lesson 7.2.3	How to authenticate sources of information for reliability. Evaluating websites and sources of information.	Comparing official and unofficial sources of information for relevance in meeting different specified criteria.
Module 2 Assignment PB page 46 TB page 47	All of 7.2	Assignment covering the same learning objectives as those covered in Module 2 lessons, but in the context of the production of a star-rating guide to using the Internet. Scope for pupils to perform at Levels 3, 4 and 5.	

Cross curricular opportunities	
Subject	Programme of study section
English 2 (reading)	4a–d (assessing information for reliability/bias)
	9b (obtaining information from ICT based sources)
Science 1 (investigating)	2d and 2e (data samples in field work)
Science 3 (materials)	2i (searching for data on burning fossil fuels)
Science 4 (physical processes)	5a (searching for information on use of energy resources)
Design and Technology	1a (searching for information)
History	4a and 4b (searching and evaluating sources)
Geography	2d (selecting information from sources)
	5a (searching for information on environment)
	6b (searching for information on tectonic activity)
	6g (searching for information on settlements)
	5d (producing and responding to ICT texts)
RE	Finding out using ICT

Unit 2.1
Information for a purpose

In this unit pupils learn how to identify whether information is relevant and suited to the intended purpose. Pupils will carry out a small survey using a questionnaire.

Supports DfES sample teaching unit 7.2.1

ICT Framework Objectives

FINDING THINGS OUT

Using data and information sources

- *Understand that different forms of information – text, graphics, sound, numeric data and symbols – can be combined to create meaning and impact.*
- *Identify the purpose of an information source (e.g. to present facts or opinions, to advertise, publicise or entertain).*
- *Identify what information is relevant to a task.*

Key vocabulary

find, identify, information, information source, locate/location, opinion/opinion poll, purpose, questionnaire, representative, sample, sample composition/size, survey, viewpoint

Suggested lesson plan

Starter
Starters 1 and 3 focus on sources of information, while Starter 2 provides a lead-in to sampling.

Main part
The first part of the unit focuses on sources of information and the purposes for which information is required. Tasks 1 and 2 allow pupils to explore these ideas. The second part of the unit introduces the topic of surveys and questionnaires which will be developed further in Unit 5. The Helpsheet, **Resource 2.1 Questions** provides help on how to write questions for a questionnaire. Task 3 helps pupils grasp that different types of questions are used for different purposes. **Resource 2.1 Cats** can be used as a focus for class teaching on sampling. The Module Task involves devising questions for a questionnaire for a holiday company called 'UWish'. Pupils select a sample and get responses to their questionnaire which they collate into a report for the company.

Resources
Pupil Book: Module 2 Unit 2.1, pages 34–37
Resource 2.1 Cats
Resource 2.1 Holidays
Resource 2.1 Questions
Resource 2.1. Survey
Variety of sources of information to be visible in room, e.g. books, magazines, CD ROMs, pictures, videos, Internet access, perhaps radio and television – these will not actually be used and are for discussion purposes only
A selection of different types of maps (sketch, Ordnance Survey, online) for discussion relating to the homework

Plenary
Review the responses to the questions in the Module Task.

Differentiation
Task 4 (Red) can be used as a 'stretch' activity for more able pupils early in the topic, or as a whole class revision of question writing and sampling.

Note: As there is a lot of material in this unit, some teachers may wish to spread it over two lessons. A suggested way of doing this is given below.

Lesson 1

Starter
Use Starter 1 or 3 to introduce the idea that sources of information are all around us and that information is used for a variety of purposes, for example to entertain, to persuade, to teach, to record.

Main part

Teach the first part of the unit on sources of information and the purposes for which information is required. Pupils do Tasks 1 and 2. Teach question writing using the Helpsheet **Resource 2.1 Questions** and Task 3. Pupils can then answer questions a and b from the Module Task, which involves devising a questionnaire for a holiday company called 'UWish'.

Plenary

Brief discussion about who to send the questionnaires to. Pupils to come up with some ideas for homework.

Lesson 2

Starter

Use Starter 2 to introduce ideas about sampling. Feed back pupil ideas from the homework about who should answer the 'UWish' questionnaire.

Main part

Teach sampling using **Resource 2.1 Cats** and Task 4. Pupils answer questions c–f from the Module Task, selecting a sample and getting responses to their questionnaire which they collate into a report for the 'UWish' company.

Plenary

Review responses to the questionnaire. Homework could be to write up the report for 'UWish'.

Suggested starters

1   Split class into groups of four or five. They are to act as research teams and need to identify the information that they would need to be able to carry out a research project. Provide them with a scenario and solution, for example: 'Research Monet's style of painting in his paintings of water lilies' Pupils have to consider the information they need and the questions they would have to ask to find answers. Other groups could look at:

   ● How do you build an igloo?
   ● What is the warmest material used to make a fleece jacket?
   ● How are drinks cans made?

The same research project title could be given to more than one group and a comparison of the sources of information carried out.

2   Whole class activity. Provide pupils with a statement: 'We live closer to New York than Moscow'. Ask for opinions as to whether this is accurate information or not. Ask pupils whether they think different age groups within the population as a whole know whether this is true, and how they would go about asking questions to test people's knowledge.

3   Whole class activity. Display an item, e.g. a tree on a whiteboard or large monitor. Ask pupils what information they could find out about the item and what they would do with the information.
For example:

   A tree
   ● Type/height etc. – planning a garden layout
   ● What it could be used for – looking at environmental projects
   ● Where trees have been featured in pictures and music – Internet.

   The purpose would be to draw out the information that would be available about items and how they can relate this to different usage.

Notes on Tasks

Task 1 (Green)

Pupils identify the sources of information that are around them within the classroom – a variety of information sources need to be visible. The pupils then have to identify the type of information that they can get from the sources. It is important that the pupils identify people, i.e. peer group and teachers, as sources as well. They are asked to consider whether the sources are reliable and which ones they could expect to trust.

Task 2 (Green)

Encourage pupils to think about issues such as how up to date the information needs to be, how long a time period it should cover, how accurate, how much detail, how wide an area, etc. Suitable sources might be websites, books, other people, maps, etc.

Task 3 (Green)

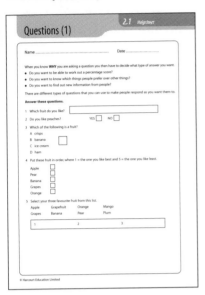

Pupils decide which types of questions would be most useful for various purposes. Suggested answers:

1 Ordered or selected questions

2 Open ended questions

3 Could be any of the closed questions

4 Yes or No questions or multiple-choice

Before tackling this task, pupils could work through the Helpsheet, **Resource 2.1 Questions**.

Task 4 (Red)

The purpose of this task is to get the more able pupils to begin thinking about issues such as context, sample sizes and the limitations of questions. Before tackling this task pupils could look at **Resource 2.1 Cats** which draws out some of the key issues about sampling.

Alternatively you could use this task as the basis for a whole class discussion on the topic, or as a revision exercise before starting the Module Task.

Module Task

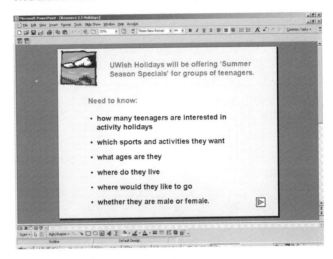

Pupils develop six questions that could be used to gather information about teenage holiday activity preferences for a fictitious travel company 'UWish'. They define a sample group, ask the questions and collate the responses into a report for the company.

The task should be introduced to the whole class using **Resource 2.1 Holidays** as a focus. It would also be a good idea to work through the Helpsheet, **Resource 2.1 Questions** with the class, prior to them starting work. Pupils should work individually or in pairs to suggest questions, using the worksheet, **Resource 2.1 Survey** as a template. In order to make this exercise practicable within one or two lessons, you may want to draw together the suggestions into one class questionnaire.

Individual pupils should make notes on the sample they would use and be able to justify their decisions. However, you may need to work with the class as a whole to turn their suggestions into a workable sample from which a response can be quickly and easily obtained. This may need setting up in advance if it requires pupils from other classes to respond.

The feedback for the 'UWish' company could be done using word processing or presentation software.

Task 5 (Green)

Pupils are asked to plan a location map of their school for visitors. They need to consider possible starting points and methods of transport that could be used as well as the visual information required. In a discussion prior to their work, pupils should be asked to list a variety of local features that could be added to their map to provide guides for visitors. The purpose of this exercise is to make pupils draw out the important pieces of information that have to be collected before being able to represent information in another form.

Homework suggestion

If you are following the two-lesson guide, pupils could undertake questions a and b of the Module Task for the first homework. If the report for 'UWish' is unfinished by the end of lesson two, pupils could complete it and/or do Task 5. It may be necessary to hold a brief discussion before the end of the lesson about the type of information needed on the map and the best format for producing one.

Suggested extension activity

As an additional activity pupils could:

1   Look at the six questions that they have written for the 'UWish' company.

2   Identify how to turn these questions into a format that could be used again and again by different companies: perhaps they have to take out some words, perhaps leave a blank in the question so words could be added in each different case.

3   Create a new series of questions which could be used to find out the following information:

How many female 14-year-olds have got brothers with skateboards?

Do all male teachers drive cars less than three years old?

Level guide

Level 5

Pupils working at Level 5 and above will make reasoned judgements about the relevance of information for different purposes. They will be able to create a series of questions that are relevant and will have the ability to extract relevant information from their results.

Level 4

Pupils working at Level 4 will identify relevant information for achieving the desired results but the information will not always have relevance. They will be able to create the series of questions but may not have selected the most appropriate for acquiring the required information. They will be able to interpret the results of the questions, and to question the plausibility of the information gained.

Level 3

Pupils working at Levels 3 and below will identify some information that they need for a specified reason. With help they will be able to create a series of questions and be able to discuss the results of the questions.

Unit 2.2
Selecting sources and finding information

In this unit pupils learn how to locate information in an efficient way.

Supports DfES sample teaching unit 7.2.2

ICT Framework Objectives

FINDING THINGS OUT

Using data and information sources
- *Identify what information is relevant to a task.*

Searching and selecting
- *Search a variety of sources for information relevant to a task (e.g. using indexes, search techniques, navigational structures and engines).*
- *Narrow down a search to achieve more relevant results.*

Key vocabulary

browse, contents list, hits, home page, identify, index, information, information source, Internet, locate/location, menu, relevant page, search, search engine, uniform resource locator (URL), web, web browser, website, World Wide Web (WWW)

Resources

Pupil Book: Module 2 Unit 2.2, pages 38–42
Resource 2.2 Web page
Resource 2.2 Sharks!
Care needs to be taken to check out any websites used are up and running prior to the lesson and where possible consider running the websites from the local network.

Suggested lesson plan

Starter
The suggested Starters help pupils to focus on the range of different sources of information, and the kinds of questions they need to ask in order to source information efficiently.

Main part
Start by reminding pupils of all the different sources of information available to them such as books, CD ROMs, other people, the telephone, email etc. Draw out questions of efficiency and the need to be precise about exactly what information is required.

This unit focuses mainly on techniques for finding information using the Internet. Pupils learn how to navigate and search for information on a website, and also how to set up and refine a search using an Internet search engine such as Google or Yahoo. The amount of demonstration needed will depend on how confident your pupils already are in navigating websites and using search engines. With pupils of all ability you should stress that the aim is to search efficiently by being as precise as possible about what information is

required. The Module Task asks pupils to search for information on a particular website.

Plenary
Draw together pupils' experiences of searching for information on the web. Was it quick, easy, successful? What were the problems they encountered?

Differentiation
Most pupils will have some ability to navigate websites. Differentiation will be around efficiency of searches and focus on the task in hand. More able pupils can be asked to find additional information which is less obviously available on the websites which are being searched. They could also be asked to synthesise the information they have found into a report, or to reflect on what they have done and suggest how they could work even more efficiently.

Suggested starters

1 Whole class activity. Each pupil is given a piece of paper on which is written a 'mystery object'. These should be

everyday items such as an electric kettle or a blackbird. The pupils must discover what is written on each others' pieces of paper. They need to work out the most effective way to get the information. Would it be by questions, drawing pictures, by people miming or roleplay? The objective is to make pupils consider more than one format of enquiry.

2   On a whiteboard or large monitor, display a route map showing the way to get to the school office from the classroom. Omit from the route map all the important 'landmarks'. Ask pupils what they think the route map shows and provide a set of options:

- School to the nearest shops
- 'X' town to 'Y' town (with X and Y being your two local towns)
- Classroom to the school office.

Ask pupils how they could find out which route the map was showing. Ask them why it is not obvious which route it displays. This should make the pupils consider the information they identified as necessary in Task 5, Unit 2.1.

3   Ask pupils to identify the best source of information to answer a wide range of different questions. For example:

- Where can you buy the cheapest A4 ring binders locally?
- What is the name of the US President's dog?
- How do you get from the school gates to Edinburgh by road?
- What are the names of the main characters in *Oliver Twist* by Charles Dickens?
- How many pupils are there attending school today?

Ask pupils to justify their suggested method of finding each piece of information.

Notes on tasks

Task 1 (Green)
Pupils identify different sources of information appropriate to different needs. They need to have an appreciation of the advantages and limitations of the different types of sources,

e.g. the Internet is only useful if you can access it and know where and how to look for websites.

Task 2 (Green)

During Module 2, pupils will be identifying the best ways to navigate their way around a series of different websites. The worksheet, **Resource 2.2 Web page**, is a good way to check that pupils know which tools to use and what the different icons on a website mean.

Task 3 (Green)
Pupils are asked to find some specific information through the use of a search engine. A selection of search engines can be accessed through http://www.heinemann.co.uk/hotlinks. This fairly simple task gives pupils practice in using search engines in preparation for tackling the Module Task in Unit 3.

Module Task

The Module Task should be introduced to the whole class. Pupils could work in pairs or individually to carry out a number of tasks related to an online resource provided by an environmentally aware aquarium. This can be accessed by going to http://www.heinemann.co.uk/hotlinks. This source of information, and the questions, could be replaced by a more locally-based source, if available. The objective is to make pupils appreciate the layout of information on web pages and how to make efficient use of tools and online features. The worksheet **Resource 2.2 Sharks!** can be used by pupils to record their answers on.

Task 4 (Red)

Although all pupils could carry out this task, it requires more intuitive use of the website. The tools and online features needed to answer the questions are available, but not highlighted, and pupils will have to find out how to get the information required.

Task 5 (Green)

Pupils are asked to plan a perfect day out for themselves and a friend. Pupils should create their ideas individually and then swap with a partner. The purpose of the task is to make them consider things from more than one point of view. For example, what they think is a good idea might be the worst thing possible to their partner.

Homework suggestion

Based on their own notes and those of their partner from Task 5, pupils should write down what information it would have been useful to have had before they started planning the day out, for example if the partner suffers from car sickness, then a long car journey is not a good idea.

Suggested extension activity

As an additional activity pupils could:

1   Create a 'Helpful Hints' sheet for a Year 6 pupil. The sheet should show the stages needed to access the Internet and a website, for example, the Cadbury website.

2   Create a bullet point list of the stages. Check that the stages work by asking someone else to use their list.

3   Ask themselves: Have they done it the most efficient way? How many stages did they need? Did their partner do it in fewer stages?

Level guide

Level 5

Pupils working at Level 5 and above will make reasoned judgements about appropriate sources of information and the most efficient way to obtain it. They will be able to identify strengths and limitations of sources for specific types of information. They will be able to navigate websites effectively and retrieve relevant rather than general information from the website. They will be able to refine searches on the Internet to gain access to specified information.

Level 4

Pupils working at Level 4 will identify relevant sources of information for achieving the desired results but the sources will not always be the most efficient way to find or receive the information. They will be able to navigate websites and find information reasonably efficiently. They will be able to retrieve a range of information from the websites, some of which may not have relevance to the subject. They will be able to use search engines to find websites but will not always get the most efficient results.

Level 3

Pupils working at Level 3 and below will identify a variety of sources of information. With help they will be able to navigate websites and retrieve information related to the subject. They will be able to make use of search engines to find information but will not make effective use of refined searches.

Unit 2.3
Assessing reliability of information

In this unit pupils learn how to judge the reliability of information.

Supports DfES sample teaching unit 7.2.3

ICT Framework Objectives

FINDING THINGS OUT

Using data and information sources
- *Understand how someone using an information source could be misled by missing or inaccurate information.*

Searching and selecting
- *Assess the value of information from various sources to a particular task.*
- *Acknowledge sources of information used.*

Key vocabulary

browse, home page, identify, information, information source, Internet, locate/location, relevant, reliable, resource locator (URL), search, search engine, uniform, web browser, web page, website, World Wide Web (WWW)

Resources

Pupil Book: Module 2 Unit 2.3, pages 43–45
Resource 2.3 Comparisons
Resource 2.3 What it says
Resource 2.3 Words
Resource 2.3 Professors
Computers with sound cards and headphones
Large screen display for demonstrations and pupil presentations
Care needs to be taken to check out any websites to be used prior to the lesson, and where possible consider running the websites from the local network.

Suggested lesson plan

Starter
Use one of the Starters to help pupils grasp the idea that they should not accept all information at face value, and that the viewpoint of the information source can radically affect the way the information is presented.

Main part
The first two tasks help pupils to appreciate that ICT makes it very easy to manipulate information to give it a different slant. Emphasise that this means they must be very careful to check the reliability of any information they are given by looking at the source, and possibly by seeking corroborating information from another source.

The second part of the unit focuses on how to check the reliability of web-based sources. Discuss the different domain names and what the underlying motivation of such sites might be and whether this could affect the reliability of the information on these sites. Point out that sometimes an unofficial site can give more useful information than an official site would – it depends on the purpose.

The Module Task and Task 3 both practise search techniques learnt in Unit 2.2, but the focus here is on assessing the quality of the information provided by different sites.

Plenary
Review learning about reliability of sources. You could mention copyright issues (covered on page 10 of the Pupil Book).

Differentiation
Suggestions are made in Task 3 (Red) and the extension task for additional searches which more able pupils could carry out. Less and more confident pupils can be grouped together for the Module Task.

Suggested starters

1   Whole class activity. Begin with a discussion to find out how well pupils can question information provided to them. Select a group of five pupils to act as 'Professors'. They are provided with information about the same subject. The information from two of them is completely false and the information from the other three all has accurate information but from different perspectives. Pupils are allowed to ask no more than two questions each to determine which are authentic sources of information and which are unreliable or need to be questioned.
Please see the Information sheet **Resource 2.3 Professors** for a sample of the type of information that the professors could have (Professors 1 and 4 are false).

2   Whole class activity. Ask pupils to write down on pieces of paper the words BELIEVE and QUESTION.

The purpose of this activity will be to develop an awareness that there are some facts that we can accept whilst there are others that need to be questioned. As a statement is made the pupils hold up either the BELIEVE card or the QUESTION card. Bring out through class discussion what needs to be questioned: it could be the facts, the source of the information or the reason for providing the information. For example:

Macbeth is the greatest play to be shown in the West End of London theatres. (Question)
The most popular breed of dog is labrador. (Question)
The Queen of England is Elizabeth II. (Believe)
The highest mountain in Wales is Snowdon. (Believe)

3   Collect together three national newspapers printed on the same day. Split the pupils into three groups, each with one newspaper to look at. Ask them to read the same news item as written in the different papers and to form an opinion as to whether they believe all of the news in the article. Make a list on the board of the points that they make about the article that they have read. The purpose of the exercise will be to make the pupils query why the articles have been written in the way that they have.

Notes on Tasks

Task 1 (Green)

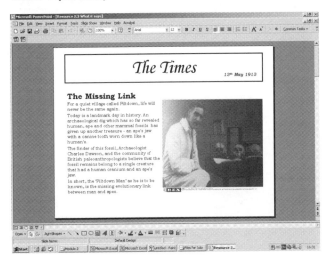

The introduction to the task should set the scene about believing or questioning everything that is presented to us. It could be used effectively as a whole class teaching activity. Pupils are asked to use **Resource 2.3 What it says** that provides them with some misleading information that was produced for different reasons. The purpose of the task is to make them consider what elements lend credibility to an information source.

Task 2 (Green)

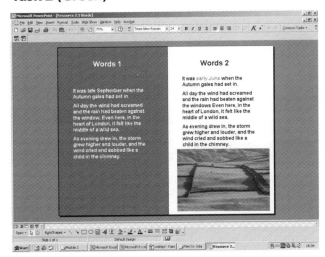

In this task pupils experience how easy it is to use ICT to edit and amend information. They access **Resource 2.3 Words**, and use their word processing skills to edit the slides and transform text from one descriptive passage into one that conveys a totally different feeling.

Module Task

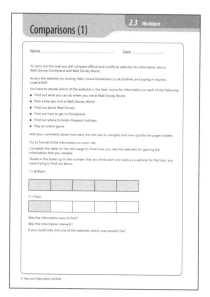

The Module Task should be introduced to the whole class. Pupils work in pairs and use the worksheet **Resource 2.3 Comparisons** to carry out a comparison between various websites. The websites chosen are all related to Disney. Some are 'official' Disney sites, others are commercial 'spin off' sites. They can be accessed by going to http://www.heinemann.co.uk/hotlinks. Pupils decide which are most suitable for a range of purposes. Care will be needed to check that the websites are accessible through the school network and that the content is felt suitable.

Task 3 (Red)

Pupils working at the higher level will be able to make value judgements about information available from two suggested websites, found at http://www.heinemann.co.uk/hotlinks. The websites provide information about Christopher Columbus and his life and travels. One is a commercially produced website, the other by an enthusiast. Pupils are asked to try to locate the sources that the website authors have used for their information as a means of checking authenticity and accuracy.

Homework suggestion

Pupils write down the names of two or three of their favourite websites and say what they use each one for and why they think it is good for that purpose.

Suggested extension activity

As an additional activity pupils could:

1 Produce a list of recommended websites for local information.

2 Use a search engine to find out:
   - the names of local theatres and cinemas
   - the names and locations of all swimming pools and leisure facilities within a 15 mile range of their school
   - the main hotels and guest houses that are located close to a shopping area.

3 Make notes about where they found the information. Do they think that the sources can be trusted?

4 Add to their list the recommended sources for information.

Level guide

Level 5

Pupils working at Level 5 and above will make reasoned judgements about the accuracy and authenticity of information found from different sources. They will understand that information may be presented to show bias towards a particular viewpoint. They will be able to refine searches on the Internet to gain access to specified information and make judgements about the authors.

Level 4

Pupils working at Level 4 will be able to identify where they need to ask questions about authenticity and accuracy of information. They will see the need to query where information comes from and that some might be biased, or have a specific angle, but will sometimes miss the way to find out the sources of information. They will use search engines to find websites but do not always get the most efficient results.

Level 3

Pupils working at Level 3 and below will be able to determine which information could be inaccurate with help. They will make use of search engines to find information but may not make effective use of refined searches.

Module 2
Stratford from the Internet

To complete Module 2 pupils are required to produce a guide to finding relevant information from the Internet.

Resources

Pupil Book: Module 2, pages 32–49

Module 2 Assignment Evaluation form

Module 2 Assignment worksheet

Word processing software

Variety of sources of information related to Shakespeare and Stratford, e.g. books, magazines, CD ROM, pictures, videos, Internet access, perhaps radio and television – these will not actually be used and are for discussion purposes only

National Curriculum Level indicators based upon pupil outcome

Level indicators At the end of this assignment		
Pupils working at Level 3 will: • Make use of the information supplied to decide upon the content of the guide • With help, use a search engine to find websites but will not apply sensible judgements as to the appropriateness of the websites for the assignment • Produce the guide without taking account of the audience • With prompting, talk about what they have done	Pupils working at Level 4 will: • Make use of the information supplied to decide upon the content and best layout for the guide • Use a search engine to locate suitable websites and copy information from the sources into their guide, without being entirely selective of the content copied • Make sure that the guide takes account of the intended audience • Discuss how they prepared their guide with knowledge of the tools and techniques developed during the Module	Pupils working at Level 5 will: • Make use of the information supplied to produce a concise and relevant guide • Check the accuracy of the information in the guide by asking others to check it • Make use of a search engine to locate relevant websites that are fit for purpose • Structure and refine the information for the intended audience • Reflect critically on the skills and knowledge they needed to produce the guide in order to make improvements to subsequent work

Module 3
Making a leaflet

Overview

Where this module fits in	Prior learning
This module builds on: Work done in KS2 POS, particularly the 'Exchanging and sharing information' section, and work done in Module 1.	To make good progress, pupils starting this module need to be able to: 1 Use basic word processing skills, including editing, inserting, deleting, moving, copying and pasting text and pictures 2 Design a simple publication by entering text and inserting pictures 3 Manipulate graphics by cropping, rotating, cutting, copying and pasting
The main concept of this module is: That images and text need to be chosen and manipulated to match the intended purpose and how images and text are used to create a corporate image involving a logo. The layout for different leaflets needs to be identified and the information adjusted to match the different layouts.	
This module leads on to: Other units that require pupils to create published documents and to manipulate text and images, for example, parts of Module 5 'Data handling'.	Revision of these areas is in Module 3 Prior learning.

Subject knowledge needed by teachers

To teach this module you will need to know how to:	Information on this aspect can be found in:
Load and save work in a shared area	Pupil Book pages 1, 24
Use graphics software to manipulate images	Pupil Book pages 57, 63, 76–77, Resource 3.5 Quality
Use a scanner and a digital camera	Pupil Book pages 29–30, Resource 3.4 Acquiring images
Access text and images	Pupil Book pages 51, 75–77
Use desktop publishing software	Pupil Book pages 50–51, 73–76
Add text and images to documents	Pupil Book pages 27–30, 51, 75–76, Resource 3.4 Graphics
Explain difference between vector-based and bitmapped images	Pupil Book page 8, Resource 3.3 Vector logos

Level indicators
At the end of this module

Pupils working at Level 3 will:
• Use ICT to generate, develop, organise and present their work
• Share their ideas with others and work in a collaborative way with partners
• Access images from different sources to enhance their work

Pupils working at Level 4 will:
• Add to, amend and combine different forms of information from a variety of sources
• Use ICT to present information in different forms and show they are aware of the intended audience
• Exchange information and ideas with others in a variety of ways

Pupils working at Level 5 will:
• Select the information that they need for different purposes
• Use ICT to structure, refine and present information in different forms and styles for specific purposes and audiences
• Exchange information and ideas with others in a variety of ways, including electronically
• Discuss their knowledge and experience of using ICT and their observations of its use outside school

Overview of module content and how it fits with the DfES sample teaching units

Module in Pupil Book	Matches DfES lesson (in terms of content and and teaching objectives covered)	Outline of content	Progress on Module Task
Module 3 Prior learning PB pages 50–51			
3.1 Creating a corporate image PB pages 52–55 TB pages 50–53	Lesson 7.3.1	Investigating why and how corporate images are used. Identifying the type of format suitable for the purpose of presenting a newsletter.	Plan template for front cover of school newsletter.
3.2 Designing a leaflet PB pages 56–58 TB pages 54–57	Lesson 7.3.2	Looking at 'good' design. Identifying areas on a publication of text and images to create a balanced layout. Working out a colour scheme for use in a publication.	Import text for front cover and create colour scheme. Import logo.
3.3 Creating a logo PB pages 59–61 TB pages 58–61	Lesson 7.3.3	Examining the use of logos and developing one for use in the specified context of the newsletter. Using a graphics program that will allow the manipulation of vector and bitmapped graphics.	Creation of a logo for a school club for use in their publication.
3.4 Capturing images PB pages 62–65 TB page 62–65	Lesson 7.3.4	Identifying where the content of the newsletter would be enhanced by adding images. Capturing and manipulating images. Creating or acquiring images through the use of a scanner or digital camera. How to crop, re-size, rotate and re-colour images as required.	Deciding on the images that will be used in the newsletter. Acquiring images with the use of digital camera and scanner and graphics software.
3.5 Improving images PB pages 66–68 TB pages 66–68	Lesson 7.3.5	Improving the images by matching the size with appropriate resolution. Altering the format of single-page layout to become two-page document.	Change layout from single-page layout to two-sided layout Change images and text to suit new space.
3.6 Creating a folded leaflet PB pages 69–71 TB pages 69–71	Lesson 7.3.6	Identifying a suitable layout for a folded leaflet, including how text and images need to be placed for accurate printing. Creating a version of a one- or two-fold leaflet.	Creation and adaptation of the newsletter into a one- or two-fold leaflet.
Module 3 Assignment PB page 72 TB page 72	All of 7.3	Assignment covering the same learning objectives as those covered in Module 3, in the context of a two-fold leaflet introducing a new facility at a leisure centre. The leaflet will be sent to all local residents. Scope for pupils to perform at Levels 3, 4 and 5.	

Cross curricular opportunities

Subject	Programme of study section
English 3 (writing)	5c (presenting information)
Design and Technology	1h (presenting designs using ICT)
Geography	1f (communicate/present data)
	6g (presenting information about settlements)
MFL	2j (creating and amending texts using ICT)
	5d (producing and responding to ICT texts)
Art	2a (using images for a purpose)
RE	Sharing ideas using ICT

Unit 3.1
Creating a corporate image

In this unit pupils learn about how design can be used to create a corporate image. They begin to plan out a cover of a school newsletter.

Supports DfES sample teaching unit 7.3.1

ICT Framework Objectives

FINDING THINGS OUT

Using data and information sources
- *Understand that different forms of information – text, graphics and symbols – can be combined to create meaning and impact.*

EXCHANGING AND SHARING INFORMATION

Refining and presenting information
- *Use ICT to draft and refine a presentation, including:*
  - *re-organising, developing and combining information, including text and images, using the simple editing functions of common applications*
  - *importing and exporting data and information in appropriate formats.*

Suggested lesson plan

Starter
Each Starter focuses on a different aspect of corporate image and prompts pupils to think about brand awareness and the appropriateness of words, images and colours for different products and contexts. This can lead to a class discussion that embraces all the important issues to consider when designing a corporate image.

Main part
Tasks 1 and 2 pursue the analysis of corporate image and invite pupils to identify the features involved in creating the image, such as logos, text styles, colour schemes and shapes. Task 4 explores the newsletter as an example of printed material that might be produced by an organisation. It introduces pupils to a desktop

Key vocabulary
audience, corporate image, design brief, desktop publishing (DTP), font, graphic(s), import, landscape, layer objects, layout, logo, object(s), organisation, portrait, re-size, shared area

Resources
Pupil Book: Unit 3.1 Module 3, pages 52–55
Resource 3.1 Corporate
Resource 3.1 Adverts
Resource 3.1 Names
Resource 3.1 Newsletter
Resource 3.1 Layers
Desktop publishing software
Collection of leaflets from a set of publications
Collection of school materials, for example, prospectus, headed notepaper, newsletter, printout of website, school photo and logo

publishing program and allows them to identify how all the elements in the document have been set up as layered objects. The Module Task takes pupils through the exercise of creating the basic design for the front cover of a school newsletter.

Plenary
For a conclusion, discuss the layout of one of the newsletter covers designed by pupils from the class. Discuss the font styles and font sizes that pupils have selected and allow the class to identify the strengths and weaknesses in the proposed cover.

Differentiation
Most pupils will be able to identify items with the same corporate image. Differentiation will show in their ability to use a desktop publishing package to set out a cover for a school

newsletter. Less able pupils will need support, particularly in the layering of elements to create the final layout. More able pupils can be asked to work out a clear outline for the cover.

Suggested starters

1 Whole class activity. Divide the whiteboard into three columns. Place a heading at the top of each column – Traditional, Everyday, Modern. Ask the pupils to vote for the type of corporate image that would be suitable for each of the following organisations/companies:

a Chain of hotels based in country mansions
b Shop that sells stationery
c Company that manufactures trainers
d Chain of fast food restaurants
e Computer superstore
f Publisher of ancient maps
g Perfume manufacturer
h Political party
i Dress design company
j School

The purpose of this activity is to make pupils consider what we accept as 'appropriate' images for certain contexts. It would be useful to be prepared with some alternative suggestions that could make pupils rethink their ideas, for example, the perfume manufacturer could fit into any of the categories.

2 Whole class discussion. Ask pupils to come up with words that could be used to describe a company that manufactures furniture from recycled materials. Start them off by suggesting a topical phrase such as 'environmentally friendly'.

Ask them for reasons why they have selected their words. Make suggestions about the type of corporate image that could come out of these words – ask what shapes, colours and textures could be used for the different items that would be used or distributed by the company.

3 Whole class discussion, followed by a paired activity. Provide a list of colours on the whiteboard covering the complete colour circle, i.e. red, orange, yellow, green, blue, purple, and add brown, black and white to the list. Ask pupils to come up with combinations of colours that are used in corporate images that they are familiar with. It is important to make them think beyond the logo, for example, Virgin has red, black and white for all branches of the company, but adds in other colours to enhance the 'feel' of the different branches. Ask them to work in pairs and try to categorise why they think the colours for the overall image and the discrete images have been chosen.

Notes on Tasks

Task 1 (Green)

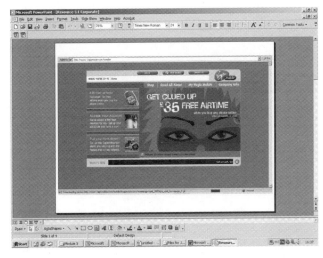

Pupils can work individually or with a partner. They look at **Resource 3.1 Corporate** which includes a range of web pages all belonging to the same company: Virgin. The web pages show slightly different uses of logos and images to reflect corporate image. Encourage pupils to give reasons why the pages are different and why the elements portraying corporate image are different on each page.

Task 2 (Green)

Pupils look at two adverts in **Resource 3.1 Adverts** and reflect on the way that the corporate image has been developed. Pupils should list aspects that are reproduced on each leaflet and ones that change. They should suggest reasons why.

Task 3 (Red)

Pupils working towards the higher levels look at **Resource 3.1 Names** to determine what kind of organisation is behind the corporate images. The three examples are taken from the logos of different banks. Some pupils may pick up that the logos are intended to reflect a 'new breed' of modern financial institutions, trying to get away from the traditional and 'stuffy' image of banks.

Task 4 (Green)

This task could be done individually, or demonstrated from the front of the classroom as a whole-class room activity. Pupils look at the layout of a sample file in **Resource 3.1 Layers** and identify how it has been set up. They examine how the text, background colours and images have been set into layers.

Encourage class discussion on the number of layers and what might be included on each layer. Ask pupils how suitable this might be for the cover of the next issue. What do they need to change? Which elements will remain the same?

Module Task

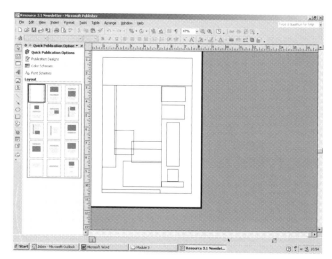

The Module Task should be introduced with a whole-class demonstration of how to set up a document template, using **Resource 3.1 Newsletter** as an example. Show the difference between text, image and background boxes by clicking on them, and demonstrate how to enter text in the text boxes and how to format it (see Skills help on page 75 of the Pupil Book). Show how to move and re-size boxes, and recap on layering. Pupils can then set up their own templates, either from scratch, or using **Resource 3.1 Newsletter** as a starting point. The elements they need to set up are those needed to create the corporate image for the school on the front page of the newsletter, including: title, school name, school logo, date, colour scheme, fonts etc.

Remind pupils of the discussion on layers and encourage them to consult the Skills help on pages 75–76 of the Pupil Book to set up text boxes and image boxes.

They should save their layout from the Module Task in the shared area and make a printout to use in the next unit.

Homework suggestion

Pupils work out a basic design using a printout of the file that they have created in the lesson. They draw on the printout where they will place the text and the different styles of text and the types of image that they will use.

Suggested extension activity

As an additional activity pupils could:

1   Look at the layout that they have worked out for the cover of a school newsletter.

2   Select the different parts of the cover necessary to create a series of different-sized publications, based around the same layout, that could be used as publicity documents.

3   These publications could include:

   a A5 flyer
   b Poster
   c Bookmark.

4   Sketch out the important corporate features that they would place on each publication.

5   Make notes about the different colour schemes that could be used to enhance the different publications and make them appear slightly different from the main newsletter.

Level guide

Level 5

Pupils working at Level 5 and above will be able to determine why and how corporate images are created and can be effective. They will be able to discuss the strengths and weaknesses of different corporate images. Pupils will be confident in working on the layout of their own publication using desktop publishing software and will understand clearly how layering of the text, images and background works. They will be able to work out an appropriate layout that provides a clear outline for the cover of a school newsletter.

Level 4

Pupils working at Level 4 will identify corporate images from a range of sources. They will understand why corporate images are used but will not always have a clear understanding of the way it differs from a company logo. They will be able to identify how to set out the cover of a school newsletter with desktop publishing software and work confidently with layering. They will make use of a template to guide them with their own design of a school newsletter.

Level 3

Pupils working at Level 3 and below will identify items that have the same corporate image. With help they will be able set out a cover of a school newsletter with desktop publishing software. They will able to use a template to place images and text and will have some understanding of basic layering.

Unit 3.2
Designing a leaflet

In this unit pupils learn about the main points of good design and how this can be incorporated into their design of the cover for a school newsletter.

Supports DfES sample teaching unit 7.3.2

ICT Framework Objectives

FINDING THINGS OUT

Using data and information sources
- *Understand that different forms of information – text, graphics, sound, numeric data and symbols – can be combined to create meaning and impact.*

EXCHANGING AND SHARING INFORMATION

Fitness for purpose
- *Apply understanding of common forms and conventions to own ICT work.*
- *Use given criteria to evaluate the effectiveness of own and others' publications and presentations.*

Refining and presenting information
- *Plan and design the presentation of information in digital media, taking account of the purpose of the presentation and intended audience.*
- *Use ICT to draft and refine a presentation, including:*
  - *capturing still images*
  - *re-organising, developing and combining information, including text, images and sound, using the simple editing functions of common applications*
  - *importing and exporting data and information in appropriate formats.*

DEVELOPING IDEAS AND MAKING THINGS HAPPEN

Analysing and automating processes
- *Use automated processes to increase efficiency (e.g. templates, master pages).*

Key vocabulary

audience, desktop publishing, draft, font, graphics, objects corporate image, import, landscape, layout, logo, organisation, portrait, re-size, shared area, white space, dpi (dots per inch)

Resources

Pupil Book: Module 3 Unit 3.2, pages 56–58
Resource 3.2 Good and bad
Resource 3.2. Plus and minus
Resource 3.2 Food
Desktop publishing software
Graphics or image manipulation software
Selection of images from the Image Bank
Collection of leaflets, flyers and other printed publications for ideas

Suggested lesson plan

Starter
The Starters provide an introduction to the basic points of good design, as well as an appreciation of the features that might change if a product is to appeal to several target audiences. They also illustrate that one element of good design is an awareness of the cost implications of the design, and another element is consideration of any other constraints that might restrict the designer's 'free hand'.

Main part
The tasks take pupils from drafting a cover design for a newsletter to realising their designs using desktop publishing software. Task 1 allows pupils to identify designs they like and dislike. In Task 3, pupils evaluate their own design against the basic criteria for good design. Once they have satisfied themselves that their design meets these criteria, they carry out the Module Task to create their cover and carry out a peer group evaluation with a partner using the same criteria.

Plenary

To draw the unit to a conclusion, involve the pupils in a class discussion on the aspects of the process that they have felt confident about and identify where they feel they need more support.

Differentiation

Most pupils will be able to create a basic design for the cover but may not take into account the balance between the separate components of the design. They may need help with the basic tools within the graphics and desktop publishing software. More able pupils will show a clear understanding of the importance of balance within their layout, providing a suitable mix of text, space and images. They will be able to use graphics software for manipulating images and a range of tools and features of desktop publishing software.

Suggested starters

1   Whole class activity. Collect together a series (at least five) of contrasting advertisements for the same type of product, for example, holiday advertisements for Walt Disney World and holidays in the Scottish Highlands. The advertisements should be the same size. Encourage a class discussion and establish which advertisements have impact. Hold up each one in turn for no longer than three seconds. Ask pupils which one they liked, and what specific features they liked and disliked. Discuss whether they think their parents, brothers, sisters and grandparents would have the same reaction. The purpose of the activity is to try to get pupils to look at features, layout and style that can appeal to different target audiences.

2   Pupils work individually followed by a whole class discussion. Display on a whiteboard or large monitor an image of a well-known tourist attraction, the London Eye for instance. Explain that they are going to have to write down a 'specification' for a leaflet that will be advertising a new feature. The pupils work in pairs to write down five points that the leaflet must contain to make it match the design that they can see. Follow up with a whole class discussion about the restrictions that can be put in place on design for corporate publications. The purpose will be to make pupils appreciate that designers do not always have a free hand to do what they would like to.

3   Whole class activity. Create several blank leaflets by folding some pieces of A4 paper in 'unusual' ways, for example diagonally. Cut some into irregular shapes and a couple with uneven edges. Ask the pupils what the problems would be if these layouts were used to create leaflets. (The main issues are the printing, production and distribution of non-standard format items.) The purpose is to make pupils appreciate that although there are benefits in using striking items, there is always a cost behind unusual items that has to be justified.

Notes on Tasks

Task 1 (Green)

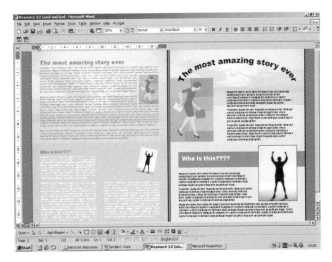

Pupils use **Resource 3.2 Good and bad** to identify the points of design that they like or dislike. Encourage a class discussion and ask pupils to answer the questions in the Pupil Book, in each case justifying their comments by identifying something on the two sample pages. The purpose of the task is to make them start to identify strengths and weaknesses in design.

Task 2 (Red)

Pupils who have confidence in the use of software programs can use this task to develop their skills in image manipulation.

They use graphics or art software, and experiment with different effects on **Resource 3.2 Food**. The manipulation can be done through the use of Paint but, if possible, other graphics software (such as Jasc PaintShop Pro) that will provide a wider range of tools and effects for the pupils should be used.
The image manipulation is an important part of the design as it can enable pupils to see how it is possible to be creative whilst still working within tight colour/layout specifications.

Task 3 (Green)

Pupils use the layout they created in Unit 3.1 together with a checklist to see if their design conforms to basic good layout. They are asked to adjust their ideas in line with the listed pointers for good design. They will make these changes in the Module Task.

Module Task

Pupils use a desktop publishing program to create their first design for the cover of the school newsletter.
They open the file they created in Unit 3.1 and make any changes as a result of the exercise in Task 3. They import the text and school logo into the correct boxes on their layout, but leave spaces for the images. You will need to ensure that an electronic version of your school logo is available for them to access.

Encourage them to save different versions of their files in the shared area to avoid losing work if mistakes are made. Suggest that they print out their best layout and discuss its features with a partner, making notes on the layout as they go.

Task 4 (Green)

Pupils first research five different logos from the Internet, magazines or newspapers. It should be stressed that they should not just pick their favourites, but a range of logos that they like and dislike. Pupils then use the worksheet **Resource 3.2 Plus and minus** to stick their cut out logos on to. They write down 3 reasons per logo to explain why they like or dislike it.

The purpose of this task is to make pupils identify why some logos are effective and why some are not.

Homework suggestion

Pupils complete Task 4.

Suggested extension activity

As an additional activity pupils could:

1   Print out two copies of their cover.

2   Cut out the separate items that they have placed onto the cover. If they need an extra copy of the cover to get all the items, then they could make a third copy. They should cut up each word separately.

3 Re-arrange the items to form a completely different layout – perhaps by changing it from landscape to portrait or the other way around.

4 Go back to the saved version of the cover and carry out the same process making use of ICT software.

5 Decide which is the easier way to make the alterations. Pupils should state the reasons why they think their chosen way is easier.

Level guide

Level 5
Pupils working at Level 5 and above will make reasoned and justified comments about the appropriateness of layout and design. They will show a clear understanding of the importance of balance within their layout, providing a suitable mix of text, space and images. They will be able to use graphics software for manipulating images and will use a range of tools and features of desktop publishing software successfully to create the cover for the school newsletter.

Level 4
Pupils working at Level 4 will identify strengths and weaknesses within differing designs. They will be able to discuss their likes and dislikes in an informed way and will be able to work out a satisfactory design that shows some ideas of balance between text, space and images. They will be confident with the basic tools and features within graphics and desktop publishing software to create the required cover for the school newsletter.

Level 3
Pupils working at Level 3 and below will be able to discuss the designs that they like and dislike but will not always make reasoned judgements. They will create a basic design for the cover but may not take into account the balance between the separate components of the design. Pupils will be able to use the basic tools within graphics and desktop publishing software with assistance.

Unit 3.3
Creating a logo

In this unit pupils learn how to design an effective logo and import it into their newsletter cover.

Supports DfES sample teaching unit 7.3.3

ICT Framework Objectives

FINDING THINGS OUT

Using data and information sources
- *Understand that different forms of information – text, graphics and symbols – can be combined to create meaning and impact.*

EXCHANGING AND SHARING INFORMATION

Refining and presenting information
- *Plan and design the presentation of information in digital media, taking account of the purpose of the presentation and intended audience.*
- *Use ICT to draft and refine a presentation, including:*
  - *capturing still images*
  - *re-organising, developing and combining information, including text and images, using the simple editing functions of common applications*
  - *importing and exporting data and information in appropriate formats.*

Fitness for purpose
- *Apply understanding of common forms and conventions to own ICT work.*

Key vocabulary

audience, corporate image, font, graphic(s), import, layout, logo, portrait, re-size, shared area

Resources

Pupil Book: Module 3 Unit 3.3, pages 59–61
Resource 3.3 Logos
Resource 3.3 Vector logos
Resource 3.3 Places
Desktop publishing software package
Graphics or image manipulation software
Selection of images, for example Image Bank
Collection of leaflets , flyers and other printed publications for ideas

Suggested lesson plan

Starter
Starters 1–3 help pupils to be inventive and encourage them to think creatively and practically about creating a logo for an organisation and for a specific product. A whole class discussion will ascertain their preferences and what they understand about logos.

Main part
Task 1 helps pupils understand how a clever and recognisable logo is vital to a successful product or brand. The Module Task focuses on creating a logo for a school club. Pupils research the use of logos in different types of context to see how they have been adapted to meet the desired requirements. They become confident in identifying what makes an effective logo. They then learn how to use the tools and features within a desktop publishing package to allow them to manipulate an image and text to make one graphic that forms a logo. Task 3 prepares the pupils for Unit 4 where they will be working on images for the newsletter.

Plenary
Pupils have the opportunity to review their work and discuss the suitability of their designed logos.

Differentiation

Most pupils will be able to create a logo for their layout for the cover of the school newsletter. Differentiation may occur when using the graphics software for image manipulation. More able pupils will have the confidence to work independently to edit and create images and import them into a file with a pre-defined layout.

Suggested starters

1 Whole class activity. Invite the whole class to look at a large circle displayed on the whiteboard. Have a brief discussion about what a circle could represent, for example the globe, a ball, a complete cycle of something, a plate or the sun. Then ask for volunteers to come up and describe how they would turn the circle into a logo for an organisation. Ask pupils to justify why they would use it in the way that they have described.

2 Split pupils into groups of four/five. Provide each group with a set of letters and ask them to come up with a logo based on the letters. Tell them that they have no more than five minutes for discussion and five minutes for creation. The sets of letters could be taken from existing companies, for example, BHS, but given in another order, such as SBH. Ask one member of each group to come out and draw the logo they have created on a whiteboard. They should also state what type of company they intend it to be. Where appropriate provide them with the 'real' version.

3 Whole class activity. Provide the pupils with an assortment of different everyday objects, each of which could be said to represent a specific context, for example a teddy bear – children; a trainer – sport; a mug – a food/drink outlet. Do not tell the pupils the context, but ask them to spend no more than five minutes coming up with an idea that makes use of the items in different logos. At the end of the time, ask for volunteers to come and draw their ideas on the whiteboard and to describe the company/organisation that they think would be able to make use of it.

Notes on Tasks

Task 1 (Green)

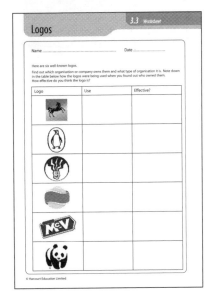

Pupils complete **Resource 3.2 Logos**. The worksheet prompts them to identify the companies who produce several well-known branded products. They are asked to find an example of the logo being used, and then to give their opinion of the logos.

The purpose of the task is to make them realise how important a clever and easily recognisable logo is to the success of a brand or product.

Task 2 (Red)

Pupils working towards the higher levels may carry this out independently but pupils working at an average level may need some support.

They use **Resource 3.3 Places** to create a letterhead and business card using images and text. The text and images are provided and the challenge comes through the sizing and placing of these resources to create the separate but themed items.

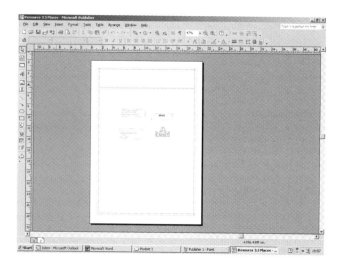

Module Task

Pupils use a software program to edit clip art images (or an image from the Image Bank) and add words to the clip to create a logo for a school club that will feature in the newsletter. They use the tools and features within the software to allow them to manipulate the image and to add text to make one graphic that forms a club logo.

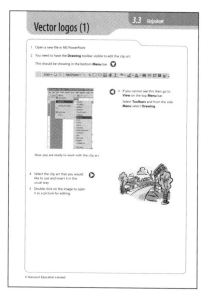

To assist them with the use of clip art images and how to manipulate them, pupils could look at the worksheet, **Resource 3.3 Vector logos**.

When they are satisfied with their created logo, they save it and make a printout. On this they can show any changes that they would like to make.

Task 3 (Green)

Pupils collect a series of leaflets and pamphlets as a source of inspiration for the images they will use in the newsletter cover design they are creating.

Help them establish ideas about the type of images that they want, the information they will use about the school, and any identifying features that form part of the corporate image. How does the text integrate with the graphics? Is there more text or images on the cover? Is there any white space?

Homework suggestion

Pupils could do Task 3.

Suggested extension activity

As an additional activity pupils could:

1 Open the file that contains their logo design.

2 Copy the logo into a graphics program.

3 Make several copies of the logo and rotate, re-size, crop or flip them so they are all different.

4 Choose a different colour scheme and apply it to the new logos.

5 For each 'new' logo state where it could be used to represent a different feature in the school newsletter – for example, it might be that the one that is rotated could represent the sports results, the one that has been enlarged could be for news of Years 10 and 11, whilst the one that has been reduced could be for news about links with primary schools.

Level guide

Level 5

Pupils working at Level 5 and above will have clear and reasoned ideas about what makes good and bad logos. They will be able to analyse the strengths of given examples. Pupils will be able to use software to create and edit images with confidence and independently. They will be able to import images into a document and adjust them to make them fit into a pre-defined layout.

Level 4

Pupils working at Level 4 will discuss the good and bad points in a sample of logos. They will be able to make use of software for image manipulation and to place the result into a document. They will also be able to create a reasonable logo for inclusion into their cover.

Level 3

Pupils working at Level 3 and below will identify differences between a sample of logos and state which they like or dislike, although they might not be able to give valued judgements. Pupils will be able to create a logo with help and copy it into their cover design.

Unit 3.4
Capturing images

Supports DfES sample teaching unit 7.3.4

ICT Framework Objectives

EXCHANGING AND SHARING INFORMATION

Refining and presenting information

● *Use ICT to draft and refine a presentation, including:*
  – *capturing still images*
  – *re-organising, developing and combining information, including text and images, using the simple editing functions of common applications*
  – *importing and exporting data and information in appropriate formats.*

Key vocabulary

audience, capture, digital camera, font, graphic(s), image, bitmapped image (bmp file), crop, design brief, import, layout, logo, portrait, re-size, shared area

Suggested lesson plan

Starter

Starters 1–3 help pupils consider how to make use of images in a publication and how to make them fit for purpose required in conjunction with any headlines and words. They concentrate on the words frequently used in headlines and that might be appropriate for their newsletter.

Main part

In Task 1 pupils consider the articles that would be in their newsletter and how these would need to be supported by the use of images. Task 2 asks pupils to alter the appearance of an image and use a range of software tools to help them. In the Module Task pupils have to make use of both a digital camera and a scanner to acquire images before manipulating, copying and pasting them into a document.

Resources

Pupil Book: Module 3 Unit 3.4, pages 62–65
Resource 3.4 Acquiring images
Resource 3.4 Articles
Resource 3.4 Word cards
Resource 3.4 Graphics
Desktop publishing software
Graphics or image manipulation software
Selection of images or Image Bank from CD ROM, including images of school or similar buildings
Collection of leaflets, flyers and other printed publications for ideas
Digital camera(s)
Scanner
Graphics software to manipulate bitmapped and vector images

A demonstration to show pupils how to use the camera and scanner equipment on the school network system might be needed.

Plenary

Consolidate pupils' experience on integrating text and images to prepare them for work in Unit 4 where they will re-work their newsletter to turn it into a two-sided A4 leaflet directed at a target audience.

Differentiation

Most pupils will be able to select images and copy and paste them between documents. Differentiation will occur in the acquisition of images from the appropriate medium (camera, scanner, clip art) for the required purpose and in the understanding of the appearance of an image within a document for a specific effect.

Suggested starters

1

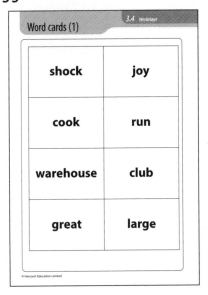

Class divided into two groups. Print off and cut up two copies of the worksheet **Resource 3.4 Word cards** to create two sets of word cards, each with a single word on it. The words fall into five categories and could be put together to make headlines. The sample words are:

shock	fright	horror
joy	happiness	laughter
cook	jump	paint
run	tighten	teach
warehouse	garage	school
club	shop	beach
great	small	minute
large	some	few
girls	boys	mice
dogs	politicians	trees

Provide each group with a set of the word cards. Pupils have to take one word from each line and create a series of headlines from them by adding in link words. For example, 'Great shock as politicians paint warehouse'. The purpose is to make pupils concentrate on the type of words that are frequently used in headlines.

2   Whole class activity. Collect a series of images and cut each of them in half. Split them into two sets and mix them up so the order of the images is different in the two sets. Split the class into two and give one set of the images to each group. A student from each group holds up the image that is on the top of the set they have. The class as a whole comes up with a suitable headline for what the 'new' composite image shows.

3   Whole class activity. Ask pupils to make a list of five television programmes, videos or films that they have watched recently. For each one ask them to list three main points of the story that they can remember. Ask them to link those three points into one headline. Select pupils to read out their headline and ask the rest of the class to state what they think the source of the headline is. Ask them to suggest the image that they would use with the headline.

Notes on Tasks

Task 1 (Green)

The images on the front cover of the newsletter will reflect various imaginary articles from inside the newsletter. This task asks pupils to think of five articles and the headlines for them which could appear on the front cover. They then identify images which could illustrate these headings. One of the headlines should be about the club for which they developed the logo in Unit 3.3. The worksheet, **Resource 3.4 Articles**, will guide pupils through this task.

Task 2 (Green)

Pupils work with graphics software (for manipulating bitmapped graphics) on an image that is used as a logo. They open **Resource 3.4 Graphics** and change the logo so that it reflects the different seasons of the year. They print off the final version of each logo and annotate their work explaining their changes and choice of colours.

Module Task

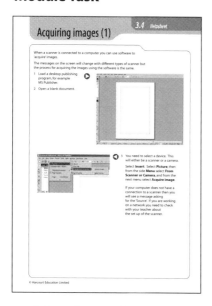

In this task, pupils acquire the images for the newsletter which they planned in Task 1. Some of their ideas may need modifying to make them practicable in the classroom. You should provide a range of printed resources from which pictures could be scanned.

Pupils use both a digital camera and a scanner. Demonstrate the use of your equipment prior to starting the Module Task and use the Helpsheet, **Resource 3.4 Acquiring images**, as reference for the pupils, adapting it to your type of equipment where necessary. Pupils load a desktop publishing program, such as MS Publisher, and open a new document file to act as a 'store' for the images they acquire. They should acquire at least one image by using a scanner and one image by using a digital camera. Other images can be obtained from the Internet or the Image Bank. Pupils then open their newsletter cover layout and copy and paste the images into the document.

Task 3 (Red)

For pupils working towards the higher levels. Although all pupils could manage this task, it is only intended for the pupils that have confidence using the sophisticated software required, and have completed the Module Task quickly.

Pupils work further with the images that they have acquired by taking them into a more advanced graphics program that allows a wide range of effects and/or colour work.

Task 4 (Green)

Pupils work out how they could rearrange their cover to become the basis of a two-sided information leaflet. The target audience is parents who may send their children to the school in future years. Pupils sketch out the layout of the new two-sided A4 leaflet and follow the same process as they did when creating the cover design.

The contents can come from the headlines and images prepared for the cover. The purpose of the change is to further emphasise the ease with which things can be changed through the use of ICT.

Homework suggestion

Pupils could do Task 4.

Suggested extension activity

As an additional activity pupils could:

1   Acquire an image from the Internet related to their local area, making sure that it is copyright free.

2   Open the image with graphic software.

3   Alter the colour scheme of the image to make it appear like an old photograph, i.e. sepia tint.

4   Use the tools available within the graphic software to delete any 'modern' items, for example cars, pylons, electric street lights.

5   Discuss with a partner the implications of being able to alter images in this way.

Level guide

Level 5

Pupils working at Level 5 and above will be able to acquire images from a range of sources and select the appropriate method for different types of image. They will be able to work on the images with confidence and incorporate them into their work checking that they are fit for purpose. They will be able to manipulate the images showing confidence and understanding about the appearance of images for specific effects or to give information.

Level 4

Pupils working at Level 4 will be able to acquire images from different sources. They will be able to acquire images using both scanner and digital camera and understand what types of image are best acquired from the different sources. They will be able to make use of software for image manipulation and will be able to copy and paste images into their documents.

Level 3

Pupils working at Level 3 and below will be able to acquire images from both a digital camera and a scanner with assistance. They will be able to change the images but may not always make them fit the purpose intended. They will be able to copy and paste images between their documents with some support.

Unit 3.5
Improving images

In this unit pupils learn how to improve the appearance of images and to place them in a two-page document.

Supports DfES sample teaching unit 7.3.5

ICT Framework Objectives

EXCHANGING AND SHARING INFORMATION

Refining and presenting information
● Use ICT to draft and refine a presentation, including:
  – capturing still images
  – re-organising, developing and combining information, including text and images, using the simple editing functions of common applications
  – importing and exporting data and information in appropriate formats.

Key vocabulary

audience, capture, digital camera, font, graphic(s), image bitmapped image (bmp file), crop, design brief, import, layout, logo, portrait, re-size, shared area

Suggested lesson plan

Starter
Starters 1–3 focus on the different types of image along with the equipment and methods necessary to make and use them. They give pupils the opportunity to consider what type of image might be best suited to a particular requirement.

Main part
Task 1 illustrates the different methods of acquiring images and their suitability for various requirements. Task 2 gives pupils practice in how the images they have acquired can be altered without affecting quality. The Module Task lets the pupils refine layouts, acquire new images, re-size and amend as needed. They re-work the contents of their newsletter cover to address the new brief by enhancing and amending the way the information is presented.

Resources

Pupil Book: Module 3 Unit 3.1, pages 66–68
Resource 3.5 Process
Resource 3.5 Quality
Desktop publishing software
Graphics or image manipulation software
Selection of images, for example the Image Bank from the CD ROM, and images of your school
Collection of leaflets (some with tear-off strips), flyers and other printed publications for ideas
Digital camera(s)
Scanner
Graphics software to manipulate bitmapped and vector images

Plenary
Review the processes in the production of the two-page leaflet, from initial stages to final form, with the whole class.

Differentiation
Most pupils will be able to move and copy images. The challenge will centre on setting up a new document from an existing one. More able pupils will have no difficulty in achieving this and may go on to explore methods of using templates, linking pages and other design features offered by the software package.

Suggested starters

1   A whole class discussion. Set out on a whiteboard (or through the use of a data projector) three columns, headed Clip Art, Camera, Scanner. Ask the pupils to give examples of which might be the most appropriate method of acquiring images might be in the following situations:

- Outdoor sports event (camera)
- Archiving family photographs (scanner)
- Add interest into a document (could be all three)
- Add images direct from software (clip art)

Ask pupils why they have chosen those sources for the best method.

2   Pupils work in groups. Ask them to list five advantages of having a digital camera. Whilst they are doing this, move around the class and take a photograph of each group. Load the photographs into a computer that can be used to display images on a large monitor or whiteboard. As the pupils provide feedback, reveal the images of the groups. This illustrates the ability to make immediate use of electronic/digital images.

3   Pupils work in groups of three. Explain to the pupils that they are going to compile a bank of photographs by using the digital camera. The photographs need to show simple scenes, buildings and a few of people. Each member of the group takes one photograph and in not more than five minutes has to make a drawing in outline of the photograph that would form an item of clip art.
Ask the group to decide on the most effective way of getting a composite image of all three of their photographs into the computer. It will involve them in arranging the images on a single piece of A4 paper and scanning it into the system. As a class, discuss the attributes of the three types of images available to them.

Notes on Tasks

Task 1 (Green)
Pupils consider the way that the different sources for acquiring images could be useful to them within their school life. They identify the advantages and disadvantages of the use of the different types of equipment.

Task 2 (Green)

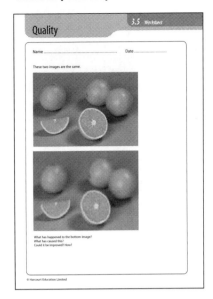

Pupils use the worksheet **Resource 3.5 Quality** to identify what happens when an image in the wrong format is stretched. They answer the questions on the worksheet. This task revisits Unit 1.2 to reinforce the difference between vector and bitmapped graphics.

Module Task
Pupils use desktop publishing software to alter their cover layout (single sheet of A4) into a leaflet (two-sheet A4 leaflet). Pupils will need their design ideas completed as homework in Unit 3.4. Using the desktop publishing software they add an extra page into their existing document file. They keep the same margins and set up text boxes to match their design ideas. Pupils add contents to the new page by copying and pasting images and text. They alter the size of the images and fonts to match the new text and image boxes. Then they delete the original (first) page.
It may be necessary to demonstrate how to add and delete pages in desktop publishing software or refer pupils to the Pupil Book Skills help, pages 74–75.

Task 3 (Red)

Pupils working at the higher level add a feature, commonly found on leaflets, to the leaflet they were working on in the Module Task: a tear-off strip. The strip consists of a dotted cutting line, a scissor graphic, fill-in lines for name, address and any other information required.

Task 4 (Green)

Give pupils the worksheet **Resource 3.5 Process** to record the process of developing the design of the newsletter cover and the production of the leaflet. Suggest they reflect on any methods of working that they would alter should they create another leaflet.

Homework suggestion

Pupils could do Task 4.

Suggested extension activity

As an additional activity pupils could:

1 Consider how the way that text is placed around images can make a big difference to the overall look of a page.

2 Select one image from their existing document and try different ways of placing text around the image. For example, the text can come close to the image or a margin can be set surrounding the image. The text could follow the shape of the image or the text could go over the top of the image.

3 Choose the text-wrapping style that they think suits the image and the layout they have created. Explain why they like this one the best.

Level guide

Level 5

Pupils working at Level 5 and above will be able to determine the different attributes of images from a range of sources. They will be able to alter the layout of their existing documents to meet the needs of the new specification. They will be able to manipulate the images to fit into the new documents and add features to make it relevant to the target audience.

Level 4

Pupils working at Level 4 will be able to identify the equipment most suitable for the production of a required image. They will be able to adjust the layout of their existing document but it may not be as well constructed. They will be able to move and alter images to fit into the new layout, although some of them will become distorted and will try to match the text and images to the intended audience.

Level 3

Pupils working at Level 3 and below will be able to discuss the different ways in which the equipment for acquiring images can be used, although their ideas may not always be sensible. With help they will able to move and copy images from their existing single-page document into their new two-page layout.

Unit 3.6

Creating a folded leaflet

Supports DfES sample teaching unit 7.3.6

ICT Framework Objectives

EXCHANGING AND SHARING INFORMATION

Fitness for purpose

- Recognise common forms and conventions used in communications and how these address audience needs.
- Apply understanding of common forms and conventions to own ICT work.

Refining and presenting information

- Plan and design the presentation of information in digital media, taking account of the purpose of the presentation and intended audience.
- Use ICT to draft and refine a presentation, including:
  - re-organising, developing and combining information, including text and images, using the simple editing functions of common applications
  - importing and exporting data and information in appropriate formats.

Key vocabulary

transfer

Resources

Pupil Book: Module 3 Unit 3.1, pages 69–71
Resource 3.6 Overlap
Resource 3.6 Folds
Desktop publishing software
Graphics or image manipulation software
Selection of images or Image Bank from the CD ROM and images of your school
A selection of folded leaflets and pamphlets to supplement those that pupils have collected
Scissors, card for display, glue, pens
Software to manipulate bitmapped and vector images

Suggested lesson plan

Starter

Starters 1–3 help pupils identify good design in a leaflet by allowing them to examine a series of different leaflets ranging from a single-folded flyer to a multi-folded map.

Main part

Task 1 lets pupils experiment on the type of layout needed to create various different folded documents. This neatly leads into Task 2 where pupils see how an A4 template can become a folded document. In the Module Task pupils create a folded document based upon their existing A4 leaflet. They add pages into the existing document, and copy and paste the items from the original pages, then delete the original. They drag and drop the images into place so the folds work. They decide if there will be 'white space' or if they will make full use of the printing area. Pupils save and print their preferred layout. They fold it to check it works.

Plenary

Task 4 could be done as a whole class discussion or as a game (like 'Going to Market...') where each pupil in turn recites the list of information points and then adds their own point before the next pupil does the same; the sooner they come up with a point the less of the list they have to remember.

Differentiation

Most pupils will be able to work within a template for a folded document but may not realise the full impact of the folds in their final design. More able pupils will be able to master the process by amending the size and orientation of images and text to fit within the folds. They may be able to identify generic stages for designing and producing leaflets.

Suggested starters

1 Whole class discussion. Write on the whiteboard (or use a data projector and computer to compile) a list of ways that folded leaflets can be made. This will act as a revision of some general terms as well as making pupils think creatively about different types of folded literature.
   Ask pupils for their ideas on folding paper to make a leaflet and to sketch what they think it could look like. For example:

   ● A4 landscape, folded down the middle, will give a long narrow leaflet

   ● square paper, folded diagonally, gives a triangle.

2 Whole class discussion with pupils in groups. Each group looks at a folded map (Ordnance Survey or similar). Look at the way in which the map is folded to fit into the cover. How are the folds arranged? How many ways does it fold? Why? Guide the pupils to identify the ease of folding it into sections so that only small sections of the map can be viewed at once if necessary, or so that squarer, larger sections can also be viewed. Ask them what they think the main advantages and disadvantages of producing items with folds might be. The purpose of the activity is to make them think about the types of items that make use of folds for functional reasons.

3 Whole class discussion. Ask pupils to think about the reasons why people make use of folded leaflets, instead of printing flat documents. List their ideas on a whiteboard. This invites pupils to think about the way that information is presented because of the folds; for example, important information can be displayed in a single exposed section – such as the title of a map. This list can be used for reference by the pupils as they carry out the Module Task.

Notes on Tasks

Task 1 (Green)

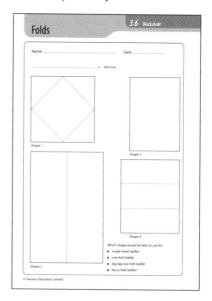

Pupils look at the worksheet **Resource 3.6 Folds** and print it out. They cut out the items and make the folds shown. They discuss their results with a partner and the possible design problems caused by the folds, for example, do you put text images across a fold? When would that not be a good idea?

Task 2 (Green)

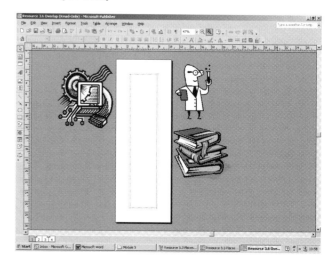

Before pupils start this task demonstrate how to set up a folded document using the software.
Pupils open the file **Resource 3.6 Overlap** and look at the **Page Setup**. This shows how to set up an image of a document so that it shows how a finished folded document will appear even though it is printed on a single side of paper. Pupils manipulate and drag and

drop images into the folded leaflet and re-size where necessary. They print and fold their document and save it with a new filename in the shared area.

Module Task

Building upon their experience in Task 2, pupils alter the layout of their two-page leaflet to a one-fold leaflet. The easiest way is to open their existing file and add extra pages, then copy and paste the images onto these pages which will become the new folded leaflet.

It is important to save the file with a new file name and only then delete the old pages. Some pupils may need several attempts before they come up with a version of the leaflet that suits the new folded layout. Pupils print out their final versions only.

Task 3 (Red)

Pupils working at the higher level continue further and make a two-fold (three-part) leaflet. This will increase the demands on their ability to manipulate text and images.

Task 4 (Green)

Pupils summarise the main points that they have considered when designing leaflets. They consider what may be a good finish to a document and illustrate this with their own leaflet.

This could be done as a whole class discussion or as a game (like 'Going to Market...') where each pupil in turn recites the list of information points and then adds their own point before the next pupil does the same; the sooner they come up with a point the less of the list they have to remember.

Homework suggestion

Pupils make notes for their files on the main points that have to be considered when designing a folded leaflet.

Suggested extension activity

As an additional activity pupils could:

1   Open their existing folded leaflet file.

2   Print out three versions of the leaflet.

3   Fold the leaflets in three 'unusual' ways to make them more appealing or to attract attention.

4   Edit their file by rotating, resizing, moving the images and/or text to make it possible to print out new versions of the leaflet with the adjusted folds.

5   Save each version of their file with a new filename in the shared area.

Level guide

Level 5

Pupils working at Level 5 and above will be able to understand and set up the layout for a folded leaflet. They will be able to place images and text so that the folds do not interfere with the layout and flow of information. Pupils will be able to alter the size of images and text to match the additional constraints of the design. They will be able to identify generic stages for designing and producing folded leaflets.

Level 4

Pupils working at Level 4 will be able to work on a layout for a folded leaflet, making use of the software tools that are there to help them (Wizards). Pupils will be able to place images and text so that the layout stays clear but may not always take into consideration the effects of the folds. Pupils will be able to identify the main stages that have to be considered when designing and producing folded leaflets.

Level 3

Pupils working at Level 3 and below will be able to work with a template for a one-fold document. They will be able to copy the images from one document to another but may not work out the full impact that the folds will have on the placed items. With help they will be able to discuss the main stages in producing a folded leaflet.

Module 3
Leisure centre

To complete Module 3 pupils are required to produce a leaflet.

Resources

Pupil Book: Module 3, pages 50–77

Module 3 Assignment Evaluation form

Access to a range of images, such as clip art and digital

photographs, or the Image Bank from the CD ROM

Desktop publishing software

National Curriculum Level indicators based upon pupil outcome

Level indicators At the end of this assignment		
Pupils working at Level 3 will: • Make use of the information supplied to decide upon the content of the document • Use basic desktop publishing tools to create a simple document, including images • Produce the document without taking account of the audience • With prompting, check spelling and layout of their document	Pupils working at Level 4 will: • Make use of the information supplied to decide upon the content and best layout for the document • Combine text and images from a range of sources successfully, making use of layering • Check the accuracy of the information in their document • Make alterations as needed to meet the specification	Pupils working at Level 5 will: • Make use of the information supplied to produce a document that matches the specification • Check the accuracy of the information in the document by asking others to check it • Locate and use images effectively creating a balance between text and images • Structure and refine the document to match specification • Reflect critically on the skills and knowledge they needed to produce the document in order to make improvements to subsequent work

Module 4

Modelling and presenting numeric data

Where this module fits in	Prior learning
This module builds on: Work done in KS2 POS, particularly the 'Developing ideas and making things happen' section.	To make good progress, pupils starting this module need to be able to: 1 Enter and amend data in a spreadsheet 2 Use letter symbols to represent unknown numbers and variables and use simple formulas 3 Describe some of the elements of a spreadsheet (e.g. cells, labels, data and formulas) 4 Use ICT to create a simple graph or chart
The main concept of this module is: To use spreadsheets to model simple situations using basic spreadsheet functions; to construct, explore and amend simple models and to consider how to manipulate graphs and tables in order to present their findings effectively.	
This module leads on to: Other units that require pupils to make use of spreadsheets and charts, particularly those in Module 5 'Data handling'.	Revision of these areas is in Module 4 Prior learning.

Subject knowledge needed by teachers

To teach this module you will need to know how to:	Information on this aspect can be found in:
Load and save work in a shared area	Pupil Book pages 1, 24
Enter formulas, numbers and labels in a spreadsheet	Pupil Book pages 78, 81–83, 105, 107 Resource 4.1 Sponsored Task Day
Copy a formula along a row or down a column	Pupil Book pages 81–82, 106–107
Understand relative and absolute cell references	Pupil Book pages 82, 107, Resource 4.1 Using absolute cell references
Sort data within a spreadsheet	Pupil Book page 85
Format spreadsheets in terms of data types and appearance	Pupil Book pages 90–91, 105–106, Resource 4.1 Calendar
Use a spreadsheet to produce graphs	Pupil Book pages 79, 97–99, 107–108
Cut and paste from a spreadsheet application into another application	Pupil Book pages 100, 110

Level indicators
At the end of this module

Pupils working at Level 3 will:	Pupils working at Level 4 will:	Pupils working at Level 5 will:
• Explore ICT-based models or simulations to help them find things out and solve problems • Generate, develop and organise their work • Follow straightforward lines of enquiry	• Explore patterns and relationships using ICT based models and simulations • Interpret their findings, question plausibility and recognise poor quality information leads to unreliable results • Present information in different forms	• Select the information that they need for different purposes • Explore the effects of changing variables in an ICT-based model • Organise information in a form suitable for processing – an increased range of quantitative and qualitative information is considered

Overview of module content and how it fits with the DfES sample teaching units

Module in Pupil Book	Matches DfES lesson (in terms of content and and teaching objectives covered)	Outline of content	Progress on Module Task
Module 4 Prior learning PB pages 78–79			
4.1 Using a spreadsheet PB pages 80–84 TB pages 75–78	Lesson 7.4.1	Identify the main elements of a spreadsheet and how to carry out simple calculations through the use of formulas. Use of basic editing tools including the use of the Fill handle tool.	Identify how and where formulas have been used in a spreadsheet. Begin to work with their own formulas.
4.2 Modelling using a spreadsheet TB pages 85–88 PB pages 79–82	Lesson 7.4.2	What is a model? Entering formulas, using sort facility to answer questions. Using 'What if…?' questions. Structure of a model.	Enter data and formulas into spreadsheet. Work out the rules and layout for a simple spreadsheet model using given data.
4.3 Building a model PB pages 89–92 TB pages 83–86	Lesson 7.4.3	Looking at rules, formulas and variables. Presentation of a model. Flexibility of models.	Setting up the rules within a model, entering data and looking at the plausibility of the results. Changing variables in models.
4.4 Refining and developing a model PB pages 93–96 TB pages 87–90	Lesson 7.4.4	Changing the rules. Checking model works after changes. Predicting outcomes.	Changing the rules of the model. Testing it still works.
4.5 Presenting data from a spreadsheet PB pages 97–101 TB pages 91–93	Lesson 7.4.5	Creating charts and graphs from a spreadsheet model. Copying and pasting tables, charts and graphs into other documents. Summarising the outcomes of a model.	Create a report from the model. Set up charts within worksheets and as separate charts. Copy and paste between applications.
Module 4 Assignment PB page 102 TB page 94	All of 7.4	Assignment covering the same learning objectives as those covered in Module 4 lessons, but in the context of setting up a model to help to assess the viability of a local community playground project. Scope for pupils to perform at Levels 3, 4 and 5.	

Cross curricular opportunities

Subject	Programme of study section
Maths 2 (number and algebra)	5f (working with formulas) 6g (working with graphs)
Science 2 (life processes)	4n (modelling changes in bacteria population) 5f (modelling build up of toxins in a food chain)
Science 4 (physical processes)	1a (modelling electric circuits)
Design and Technology	1g (modelling time/costs of design projects)
History	4a and 4b (searching and evaluating sources)
Geography	2g (modelling for decision making) 6j (modelling effects of transport on environment) 5d (producing and responding to ICT texts)
PE	9 and 10 (modelling performance rates)

Unit 4.1
Using a spreadsheet

In this unit pupils learn how to use spreadsheets.

Supports DfES sample teaching unit 7.4.1

ICT Framework Objectives

DEVELOPING IDEAS AND MAKING THINGS HAPPEN

Models and modelling

● *Use software to investigate and amend a simple model by:*
  – *formatting and labelling data appropriately*
  – *entering rules and formulas.*

Key vocabulary

absolute cell reference, address, cell, cell reference, column, cut, data, drag, formula, graph, label, model, paste, relative cell reference, value, variable

Suggested lesson plan

Starter

Each Starter involves a class discussion on the use of spreadsheets and the basic structuring of a worksheet into rows, cells, and columns. The terminology of cell references and addresses can be emphasised.

Main part

Task 1 involves pupils in a paper-based exercise calculating the cost of ordering tickets for several shows. They then compare this to a worked example using a spreadsheet, noting the formulas used and the answers obtained. Task 2 allows pupils to make use of the automated sequencing facility and the **Fill handle** tool to generate a personal calendar for 2003. The Module Task shows a prepared spreadsheet for pupils to examine. They also have the opportunity to set up the formulas in the spreadsheet and obtain a set of answers. This completed spreadsheet will be used by them in subsequent units throughout the module.

Resources

Pupil Book: Module 4 Unit 4.1, pages 80–84
Resource Sheet 4.1 Show stoppers
Resource 4.1 Extra
Resource 4.1 Calendar
Resource 4.1 Shows
Resource 4.1 Sponsors
Resource 4.1 Sponsored Task Day
Resource 4.1 Using absolute cell references
Spreadsheet software
Calculators

Plenary

For a conclusion, a discussion on the advantages and disadvantages of using a spreadsheet will provide the opportunity for pupils to consolidate their knowledge of spreadsheets.

Differentiation

Most pupils will be able to identify where formulas have been used in a spreadsheet and explain what the formulas do. They will be able to work out where formulas could be used and present them in the correct format. They will be able to enter data into a prepared spreadsheet and understand the common terminology used to describe the elements of a spreadsheet. More able pupils will be able to go on to explain why absolute cell references are used and apply the correct formulas to carry out calculations.

Suggested starters

1   Whole class discussion. Use a simple word game to introduce the terminology related to spreadsheets. Display illustrations that give a second meaning to the elements and ask pupils what they think these elements are in a spreadsheet:

cell   (illustration could be of a prison cell or biological cell)

column   (illustration of a Roman column)

row   (illustration of a rowing team)

2   Class works in groups of four or five. Ask each group to come up with ideas as to where they think spreadsheets are used (banks and finance departments). Prompt if necessary. Ask each group to give you a list of five things that they think spreadsheets can do. Make a list for the class and add to it the work that they will be doing with spreadsheets, for example 'What if…?' questions. Ask them where they think 'What if…?' questions could be used and how the spreadsheets would be different from those used by organisations and companies. The purpose of the activity is to make pupils realise that although the calculations and spreadsheet models used commercially might be complex, essentially they perform the same operations as those in the home.

3   Whole class discussion. Ask each pupil to think of a number, and then double it (without a calculator) and at the same time enter the number into a spreadsheet. Create the sequence and use the **Fill handle** tool to generate the automated doubling sequence of the number. Show the process on a large monitor, whiteboard or data projector. Ask pupils to give you another number and repeat the process until understood.

Notes on Tasks

Task 1 (Green)

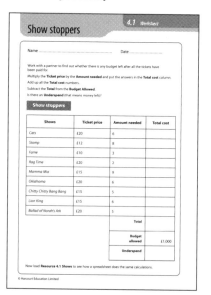

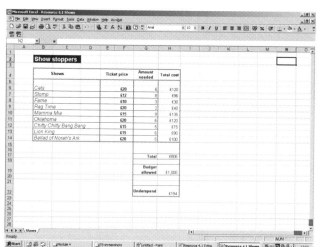

Pupils use the worksheet **Resource 4.1 Show stoppers** and with calculators answer the questions about the bookings and number of tickets required. Then they look at **Resource 4.1 Shows** which shows a worked example using a spreadsheet. It shows the formulas used to carry out the task and the expected results.

Task 2 (Green)

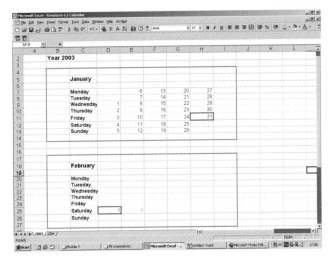

Pupils use the **Fill handle** tool in **Resource 4.1 Calendar** to generate a calendar for 2003. They complete the month of February first as this has been started and then continue in the same way for the whole year. Remind them that 2003 is not a leap year.

Module Task

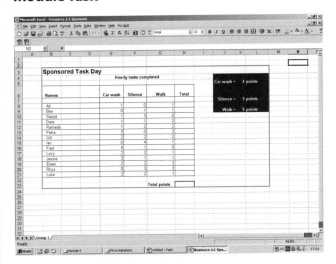

In the Module Task, pupils first write down the formulas needed to complete the spreadsheet. There is also a worksheet, **Resource 4.1 Sponsored Task Day**, which asks pupils to calculate the totals manually. You may wish to use this with less-able pupils before tackling the Module Task. Pupils then open the spreadsheet in **Resource 4.1 Sponsors** and complete it using the formulas they have worked out. They can also practise using the **Fill handle** to copy the formulas.

Task 3 (Red)

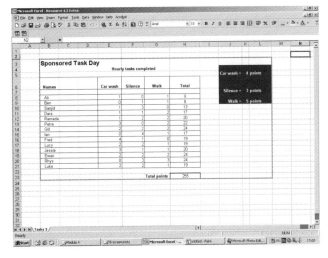

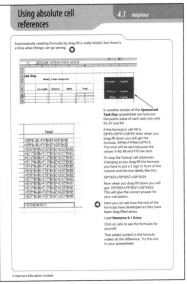

Pupils working at the higher level examine a second version of the spreadsheet from the Module Task in **Resource 4.1 Extra** with the formulas entered in a different format. This will introduce them to the basic concept of absolute cell reference and the use of the $ symbol within a formula. Provide pupils with the Helpsheet **Resource 4.1 Using absolute cell references**.

Task 4 (Green)

Pupils consider the advantages and disadvantages of using a spreadsheet. Advantages include not having to carry out repetitive calculations or the tedious task of entering data. Disadvantages include having to have access a computer and setting up the spreadsheets.

Homework suggestion

Pupils could complete Task 4.

Suggested extension activity

As an additional activity pupils could:

1   Look at the formulas that they have decided need to be used in the 'Sponsored Day' Task.

2   Explain what happens to the cell references in the formula on each of the rows.

3   Work out what the formula would be if there were more names added and the formulas went down as far as Row 26.

Level guide

Level 5

Pupils working at Level 5 and above will be able to identify where and why formulas have been used in a spreadsheet model. They will be able to identify the elements of a spreadsheet and add data to a prepared spreadsheet. They will be able to explain why absolute cell references are used and to apply the correct formulas to carry out calculations. They will able to identify strengths and weaknesses in using spreadsheets.

Level 4

Pupils working at Level 4 will be able to identify where formulas have been used in a spreadsheet and explain what the formulas do. They will be able to work out where formulas could be used and present them in the correct format. They will be able to enter data into a prepared spreadsheet and understand the common terminology used to describe the elements of a spreadsheet. They will appreciate the advantages of using a spreadsheet when discussing what they have done during the tasks.

Level 3

Pupils working at Level 3 and below will work with assistance to enter formulas into a prepared spreadsheet. They will be able to explain what is happening to the data but may not always work out new formulas. Pupils will be able to identify some advantages in using a spreadsheet.

Unit 4.2
Modelling using a spreadsheet

Supports DfES sample teaching unit 7.4.2

ICT Framework Objectives

DEVELOPING IDEAS AND MAKING THINGS HAPPEN

Models and modelling

- Use software to investigate and amend a simple model by:
  - formatting and labelling data appropriately
  - entering rules or formulas and checking their appropriateness and accurate working
  - explaining the rules governing a model.
- Test whether a simple model operates satisfactorily.

Key vocabulary

interrogate, output, predict, simulate, variable

Suggested lesson plan

Starter

The Starters make pupils consider the usefulness of models and the variety of situations in which they can be used.

Main part

As part of the wider understanding about what spreadsheet models can be used for, pupils carry out Task 1 and answer questions that need them to use the sort facility. They use the model to find information from the data. Task 2 requires pupils to interrogate a model with a set of 'What if...?' questions. They can then move on to a model in the Module Task and investigate how it has been set up. They examine the way the formulas have been used and see how the layout has been improved over several stages of development. Pupils carry out revised calculations and find the solution to a different range of questions. It might be appropriate to use the Module Task as a teaching point to demonstrate how to add columns and amend data in a spreadsheet. The questions could be answered as a whole class discussion.

Resources

Pupil Book: Module 4 Unit 4.2, pages 85–88
Resource 4.2 Sorting
Resource 4.2 Planning a model
Resource 4.2 Groups
Resource 4.2 Updates
Resource 4.2 Show more
Resource 4.2 What if
Spreadsheet software
Calculators

Plenary

Task 4 identifies the three main elements of a model so that pupils can begin from scratch. Bring their work in this unit together by discussing a particular scenario and what information might be needed to develop a model from scratch.

Differentiation

Most pupils will understand that computer models can be used to help work out solutions for problems and to predict possible outcomes. They will be able to use a basic model to answer simple 'What if...?' questions and carry out routines to order and sort the data within columns or rows. Whereas some pupils will be able to organise their ideas for creating their own model, more able pupils will be able identify the main elements of information that they will need to develop it. They will show an understanding of what should be done at a computer and what preparation work should be done away from it.

Suggested starters

1 Whole class discussion. Ask pupils how they think a computer-based model could be useful in the following settings:

  a mail order company

  b train company

  c theatre company.

The purpose of the activity is to make pupils consider the usefulness of models and the variety of situations in which they could be used. For example, to identify trends in sales; to look at the number of passengers on different train journeys in order to predict the rise and fall in passengers at different times of the year; to monitor the sale of theatre tickets and to predict if more performances are needed.

2 Whole class discussion. Ask pupils what they think would happen if someone at the Bank of England put the wrong value into a spreadsheet model used to work out the value of the pound sterling. Although a bit far-fetched, the purpose of the activity is to make pupils consider the importance of the models that are used by the Treasury and Bank of England. Ask pupils how they think errors like this are avoided.

3 Whole class discussion. Ask pupils to think how supermarkets know what stocks of sandwiches or loaves to have in the stores each day. (By studying previous sales of sandwiches and loaves.) Ask them where else they think models to work out trends might be set up.
The purpose of the activity is to make pupils start to think about 'What if…?' scenarios.

Notes on Tasks

Task 1 (Green)

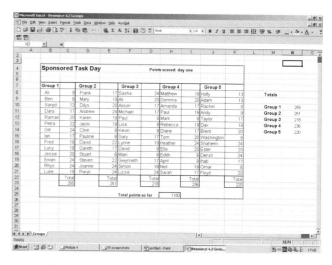

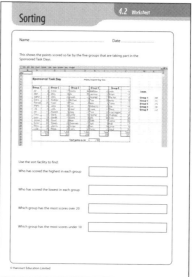

Pupils look at **Resource 4.2 Groups** and answer the questions to show they can interpret the spreadsheet. They record their answers on the worksheet, **Resource 4.2 Sorting**.

Pupils can use the Skills help section on page 137 of the Pupil Book or a demonstration of the **Sort** facility could be given on a large monitor or whiteboard.

Task 2 (Green)

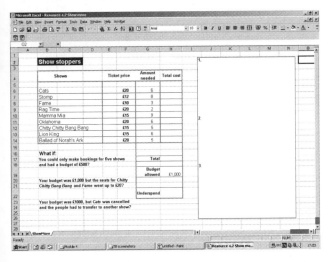

Pupils work on **Resource 4.2 Show more**. They enter the formulas that they worked out in Task 1 of Unit 4.1 and then use the model to work out the answer to three 'What if...?' scenarios. Answers can be typed in the text box, or written down if preferred.

Give them **Resource 4.2 What if** that shows a worked example that they can compare with their own spreadsheet. The task allows them to see if their formulas have been successful and to begin to see how spreadsheets can be used to model situations.

Module Task

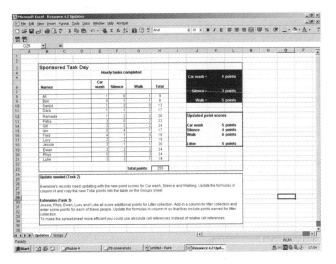

The Module Task involves looking at a What if...? scenario for the Sponsored Task Day.

Pupils open **Resource 4.2 Updates** and use the new information to update the formulas and calculate a new set of results. They then sort the results and save their work.

Task 3 (Red)

Pupils open their 'Updates' file from the Module Task and save it with a different filename. They incorporate new information (on litter collection) and use absolute cell references. They update formulas and obtain a new set of results with the new information.

Task 4 (Green)

Pupils explain the three main elements of a model. They use the worksheet, **Resource 4.2 Planning a model** to help them. They think about the design of a model using a computer and without using a computer. The purpose of the task is to make pupils consider areas that will be taken up in the next unit.

Homework suggestion

Pupils could do Task 4.

Suggested extension activity

As an additional activity pupils could:

1 Open a new spreadsheet file.

2 From **Format** drop down menu select **Cells** and look at the different ways they can alter the appearance of a spreadsheet.

3 Set column A to be red, column B to be blue. Then select individual cells and change the border and colours.

4 Select a font to use and add some text into a range of cells. Change the font style, size and alignment of the text in the cells.

5 Save this file in the shared area.

Level guide

Level 5

Pupils working at Level 5 and above will be able to identify how spreadsheet models can be used to predict outcomes or model behaviour. They will be able to use a spreadsheet model to answer 'What if...?' questions. They will be able to use the sort facility to order data across a range of cells in order to answer questions, and to organise the stages and requirements for setting up a model of a situation. They will show an understanding of what should be done at a computer and what preparation work should be done away from it.

Level 4

Pupils working at Level 4 will understand that computer models can be used to help work out solutions for problems and to predict possible outcomes. They will be able to use a basic model to answer simple 'What if...?' questions. They will carry out sort routines to sort the data within columns or rows. They will be able to organise their ideas for creating their own model and will be able to identify the main elements of information that they will need to develop it. They may not always work efficiently by planning away from the computer.

Level 3

Pupils working at Level 3 and below will see how spreadsheet models are used to model situations and predict outcomes. With help they will be able to answer simple 'What if... ?' types of question and can be encouraged to identify the information that is required to set up a new model.

Unit 4.3
Building a model

In this unit pupils learn how to create a spreadsheet model of a situation.

Supports DfES sample teaching unit 7.4.3

ICT Framework Objectives

DEVELOPING IDEAS AND MAKING THINGS HAPPEN

Models and modelling

- Use software to investigate and amend a simple model by:
  - formatting and labelling data appropriately
  - entering rules or formulas and checking their appropriateness and accurate working
  - explaining the rules governing a model.
- Test whether a simple model operates satisfactorily.

Key vocabulary
There is no new vocabulary in this lesson.

Resources
Pupil Book: Module 4 Unit 4.3, pages 89–92
Resource 4.3 Design
Resource 4.3 Rules
Resource 4.3 Week
Resource 4.3 Day
Resource 4.3 Framed
Spreadsheet software

Suggested lesson plan

Starter
Each Starter focuses on a different aspect of the three elements involved in setting up a model using spreadsheet software: rules, formulas and variables. Pupils are prompted to think carefully about these parameters as they roleplay some examples.

Main part
Task 1 follows on the theme of rules, formulas and variables and allows pupils to explore a model of a worked example.

In Task 2 pupils have to enter data and variables into the spreadsheet model and look to see if the results are sensible. The model is being used as a predictive tool. As a continuation of the investigation of models Task 3 shows the stages in development of a working model. Then in the Module Task pupils have the opportunity to add data to the model. They use appropriate software tools to add more data and expand the functionality of the model. In Task 5 pupils have to consider what the implications are for adding more data into the model.

Task 4 is more appropriate for pupils working at the higher level. They manage two significant changes to the model. One change requires them to move and add data, whilst the other alters variables and therefore the results of running the model.
A demonstration to show how these alterations are made (by using a data projector) may be beneficial for the whole class and lead to a fruitful class discussion.

Plenary
Pupils need to reflect upon the way the extended model now performs.

Differentiation
Most pupils will be able to work out what rules are needed to make a spreadsheet model work effectively. The ability to use formulas to make a model work may vary. The more able pupils will be able to work out formulas to obtain the results and discuss the implications for the change in variables. They will realise the importance of checking that their results are sensible after having made alterations to the model. They will be able to amend the structure of a model to cope with changes.

Suggested starters

1 Whole class discussion. Explain the three elements that pupils need to be able to work with in a spreadsheet model, i.e. **rules**, **formulas**, **variables**. Use roleplay to illustrate why these three elements are important. For example, ask for two volunteers to come to the front of the class. Instruct them to stand on one leg, not touching each other – these are the rules (1 and 1). To make them feel a bit safer, tell them that they can hold hands – this can represent a formula (= 1+ 1) Now change the **variable** for one of the pupils by letting them stand on both legs – so the model has changed (to 1 + 2). Ask the pupils what types of rules they think need to be put in place and how the formulas and variables need to work with these rules.

2 Class works in three groups.
A spreadsheet model is to be set up to find out which group of pupils has made the most improvement in their speed for running the 100 metres. Each group is to come up with the information that is needed to set up the model. Group 1 has to identify the **rules**, i.e. what the model must do and must not do. Group 2 has to come up with the **formulas** and tools that will be needed to make the model work. Group 3 has to list the **variables** that they think will be needed. After not more than 10 minutes ask the groups to provide the information for the rest of the class. There may be some issues that have to be resolved, for example the rules might contradict the formulas.

3 Whole class discussion. Ask the class to come up with a situation that they think could make use of a model, and make some suggestions that they expand upon. For example, weather, time for journeys, cost of holidays, nutrition. Select one and ask the class to discuss what they would want the model to do. Direct the discussion down the route of identifying the rules, formulas and variables that would be needed for their model.

Notes on Tasks

Task 1 (Green)

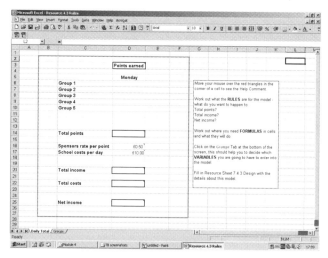

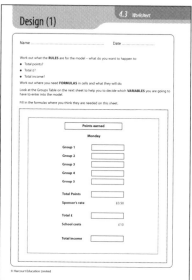

Pupils look at **Resource 4.3 Rules** which shows a spreadsheet of five groups of pupils involved in the Sponsored Task Day.

They complete the worksheet **Resource 4.3 Design** to record their ideas about the rules, formulas and variables that have been used in the prepared spreadsheet.
The task draws on pupils' ideas from Task 4 in Unit 4.2 and shows data from a real-life situation.

Task 2 (Green)

Pupils enter data into the spreadsheet model in **Resource 4.3 Day**. They make use of the **Fill** and **Copy** and **Paste** tools to familiarise themselves with the process.

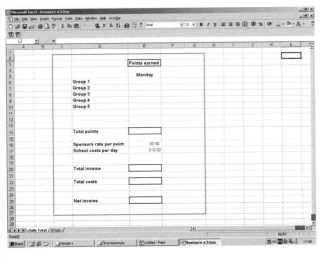

There are two worksheets in this file; start by clicking (at the bottom of the screen) on the 'Groups' tab and then move to the 'Daily Total' tab. It may be worth going over the use of absolute cell references and the way formulas are set with the pupils, to refresh their memories.

Task 3 (Green)

This task focuses on the stages in developing a model and in particular, on presentation issues. Pupils look at the model spreadsheet in **Resource 4.3 Framed**. The model has been developed in three stages.
They click on the 'Formulas' tab first, then the 'Layout' tab and then on the 'Final' tab.

Each stage improves in layout and function. Pupils make notes about the way the layout of the worksheets changes, for example the type of font, font styles, pictures, alignment, cell width.

Module Task

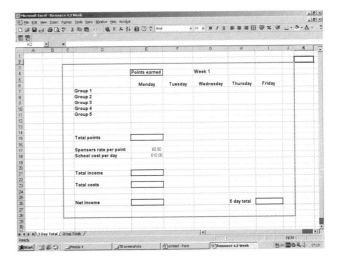

Pupils make the model more complex but also more realistic. They open the spreadsheet in **Resource 4.3 Week** and enter data for the whole week in a similar way to the data they entered for a single day in Task 2 for the Sponsored Task Day. They complete the week's worth of data for all five groups. They should be encouraged to use the appropriate tools of **Fill Down** and **Fill Right** to copy the formulas, where possible. They may need reminding that the school cost is a per-day cost and will need multiplying by the number of days.

Task 4 (Red)

This task gives more able pupils the opportunity to consider what the implications are of adding more data into the model. They are asked to make two significant changes to the model. In the first case the layout of the model will have to be reworked. This could affect the formulas so pupils will need to check their model to make sure that the formulas are still producing sensible results. In the second case, a variable is changed that has an effect on the results from the calculations.
NB It is important that these pupils save their work from this task with a different filename, as they will need to go back to the version that they saved at the end of the Module Task, in order to do the tasks in unit 4.4.

Task 5 (Green)

Pupils look at their saved file from the Module Task carried out on the Sponsor Scheme. They identify problems that might occur by continuing the scheme for another week using the same model. For example, issues of complexity: where to put all the data, having to move between lots of different worksheets, the effect on any results obtained. Possible solutions could include summarising/ totalling information or using the paste link facility in Excel.

Homework suggestion

Pupils could do Task 5.

Suggested extension activity

As an additional activity pupils could:

1   Open their latest saved version of the spreadsheet for the Sponsor Scheme.

2   Look at the way that the data is being used within the model.

3   Work out if there is a model that could be created to save having to paste between the different worksheets.

4   Ask: could the same formulas be used to calculate the Group Total instead of copying and pasting from the Daily Total?

5   Give their reasons for adding formulas to calculate the Group Total or keeping the model in the format that is used for the Daily Totals.

Level guide

Level 5

Pupils working at Level 5 and above will be able to set accurate rules for how a spreadsheet model should function. They will be able to work out formulas to obtain the results and discuss the implications for the change in variables. They will make use of software tools and techniques to improve their efficiency. They will realise the importance of checking that results are sensible after having made alterations to the model. They will be able to amend the structure of a model to cope with changes.

Level 4

Pupils working at Level 4 will be able to work out what rules are needed to make a spreadsheet model work effectively. They will be able to use formulas to make a model work although the formulas used may not be the most efficient ones. They will be able to use basic software tools to add data efficiently and understand the need to check that the model is working properly after making changes.

Level 3

Pupils working at Level 3 and below will understand that rules are necessary to make a spreadsheet model work effectively although they may not generate any original ones themselves. They will be able to add formulas to the model with assistance and explain what the formulas will do. They will use software tools to add data into the spreadsheet and when prompted will be able to check that the model still works after changes have been made.

Unit 4.4
Refining and developing a model

Supports DfES sample teaching unit 7.4.4

ICT Framework Objectives

DEVELOPING IDEAS AND MAKING THINGS HAPPEN

Models and modelling
- *Use software to investigate and amend a simple model by:*
  - *entering rules or formulas and checking their appropriateness and accurate working*
  - *predicting the effects of changing variables or rules.*
- *Test whether a simple model operates satisfactorily.*

Key vocabulary
There is no new vocabulary in this lesson.

Resources
Pupil Book: Module 4 Unit 4.4, pages 93–96
Resource 4.4 New rules
Resource 4.4 Changes
Resource 4.4 Expenses
Module 4 Worked example – for teacher only
Large computer screen display
Spreadsheet software

Suggested lesson plan

Starter
The Starters focus on introducing a variable into a working model. This gives the pupils the chance to think about the implications of introducing a variable, the expected results and therefore, the rules for a new model.

Main part
In Task 1 pupils work with a new set of rules for the Sponsor Scheme model that will increase the amount of money that can come from sponsors. They work out the new formulas for the new rules and plan the layout for the new model to take account of the changes.

In Task 2 pupils have the opportunity to try out their new version of the model. They add a variable and move data around to meet the new rules. In the Module Task they add further variables and test the results to check the viability of the model.

The purpose of the task is to make pupils appreciate the complexity of models.

A class discussion should bring out the difficulties of creating a new model by adding variables. Task 3 challenges pupils to come up with solutions.

Plenary
In Task 4 pupils identify the different ways they could present data and establish what data they might need to put into a report to sponsors. They work out how they will find the data and the best format for it to be presented.

Differentiation
Most pupils will be able to work out what would happen if rules within a spreadsheet model are changed. Some may need assistance to change a model to introduce new rules and make use of software tools to help them enter data. More able pupils will be able to set up a model showing efficient use of software tools and techniques. They will have the confidence to try to find out faster and more economical ways of copying and pasting data between files.

Suggested starters

1 Whole class discussion. Describe a situation where the ability to change the rules that apply to a spreadsheet model can be an advantage. For example, a company makes use of a predictive model to decide what type of magazines most people buy when they are going on a journey. They have a total limit for a magazine of 1,000 sales per day to be included in the model. Ask the pupils what the company should do to the sales level if they wanted to increase the range of magazines but still keep sensible stock levels. Make it higher or lower?

2 Pupils work with a partner. Give pupils not more than five minutes to come up with a list of five rules for a model to show the time pupils can spend on homework during the year. Ask them to work out what the rules should be and what information they would have to get from the school before the rules could be put in place. Explain that the rules might need to change at any time. Compile a list of their ideas on a whiteboard for all the class to share.

3

Whole class discussion. Display **Resource 4.4 Expenses** on a large monitor or whiteboard. Ask the pupils to explain what the consequences would be if Rule 1 changed to £0.35 per mile travelled.

Notes on Tasks

Task 1 (Green)

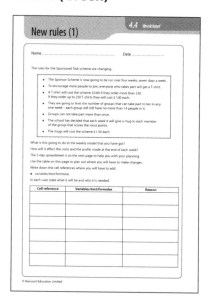

The rules for the Sponsor Scheme model that pupils have been using are going to change. Give them the worksheet **Resource 4.4 New rules** that includes the new set of rules that they have to use on the model, a worksheet to plan out the changes, and a sample spreadsheet for the new model to help them with the task.

NB Pupils who did Task 4 in Unit 4.3 should go back to the version before they did that task, in order to do their planning.

Task 2 (Green)

Pupils add a new worksheet to their file and copy the model into it to create a 'Testing' worksheet. They enter test data into this 'Testing' worksheet without affecting the existing model. The test data should be very simple round numbers, such as 1 or 10, so that pupils can easily check the totals are correct. Suggest they work with a partner to check the results (this is an important aspect of the development of the model). They should ask their partner to try out their model and they should try out their partner's model.

It is advisable to demonstrate how to add an extra worksheet to the model by using a large monitor or whiteboard, or refer pupils to Skills help on page 104 of the Pupil Book.

Module Task

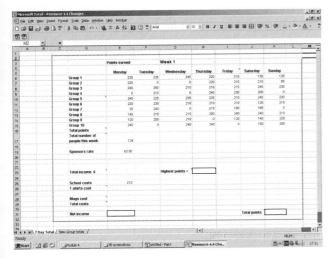

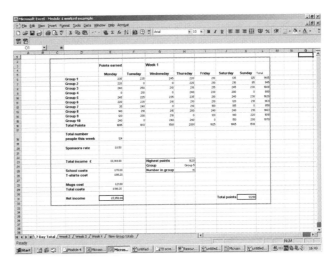

Before starting the Module Task make sure pupils are confident in changing rules and data within a model. Remind pupils that they will need their plans from Task 1 for the Module Task. They check their plan against the Sponsor Scheme model in **Resource 4.4 Changes**. This prepared file provides comments that will help them to work out what they have to do to make the changes to the model. The comments are attached to cells marked with a red triangle. Holding the mouse over them makes the comment pop up. If their plans match the comments, they can proceed. If their plans vary, ensure that they rework their plans and are satisfied that they understand the changes. They open the last saved version of their model and make the changes.

NB Pupils who did Task 4 in Unit 4.3 will need to go back to the version *before* they did that task.

The data they need is available on the 'New Group Totals' worksheet of **Resource 4.4 Changes**. On completion pupils should have four worksheets with data for seven days contained in each worksheet. There is a worked example in the Teacher-Only Resource folder on the Resource Bank CD ROM **Module 4 Worked example**.

Task 3 (Red)

Pupils working at the higher level try to find out if there is a software setting that can help them when copying data between two worksheets. (If they select **Window** and **Arrange**, they can have both worksheets open and copy and paste data between them. They can colour code different worksheets and groups.) See Skills help on pages 103–104 of the Pupil Book.

Task 4 (Green)

Pupils begin to plan the report that they are going to create for the sponsors. A class discussion about different methods of presentation should bring out the use of tables and charts to make numerical data easy to understand and interpret. They make a list of the ways they can find information about the best performance. (They can find this by carrying out sort routines, as covered in Unit 4.2.)

Homework suggestion

Pupils could do Task 4.

Suggested extension activity

As an additional activity pupils could:

1 Open the latest saved version of their Sponsor Scheme spreadsheet file.

2 Add an additional worksheet into the file. Rename this worksheet 'Stars'.

3 Set the sheet to a colour of their choice and set the font to one that is large enough to stand out.

4 Label cells with the group numbers (Group 1–Group 10) and enter a description of each of the group's best performance by examining each Group Total in the Group Data worksheet in **Resource 4.4 Changes**. For example, Group 5 'hits the jackpot' with 1620 points in Week 1.

5 Save this version of their work with a different filename.

Level guide

Level 5

Pupils working at Level 5 and above will be able to discuss the implications of changing rules within spreadsheet models. They will predict with confidence the results of changes to rules and variables within a model. They will set up a model showing efficient use of software tools and techniques. They will have the confidence to try to find out faster and more economical ways of copying and pasting data between files. They will be able to discuss the different methods of presenting data to make it more accessible for others to understand, including graphs and charts, and will also understand that the different presentation methods include material in electronic format.

Level 4

Pupils working at Level 4 will be able to work out what would happen if rules within a spreadsheet model are changed. They will be able to change a model to introduce new rules and make use of software tools to help them enter data. They will be able to describe different methods of presenting data to others including the use of charts and graphs.

Level 3

Pupils working at Level 3 and below will follow what happens when the rules in a spreadsheet model are changed. With assistance they will be able to change the data in a model to allow for rule changes. They will be able to show an appreciation that data can be presented in more than one form, and read data from graphs and charts.

Unit 4.5
Presenting data from a spreadsheet

Supports DfES sample teaching unit 7.4.5

ICT Framework Objectives

DEVELOPING IDEAS AND MAKING THINGS HAPPEN

Models and modelling

- Use software to investigate and amend a simple model by:
  - formatting and labelling data appropriately
  - entering rules or formulas and checking their appropriateness and accurate working
  - explaining the rules governing a model
  - predicting the effects of changing variables or rules.
- Test whether a simple model operates satisfactorily.

Key vocabulary
template

Resources
Pupil Book: Module 4 Unit 4.5, pages 97–101
Resource 4.5 Charts
Spreadsheet software
Word processing software or desktop publishing software

Suggested lesson plan

Starter
The Starters ask pupils to identify the different forms of presenting information. They then discuss how and where they think the different types of information are appropriate to the data. They are asked to find out which forms would be best for specific purposes, for example to show data as a percentage.

Main plan
In Task 2 pupils convert the data within their model into charts and graphs. They save them in different forms and add them into new worksheets in the file or as items within the spreadsheet. In the Module Task pupils copy and paste their tables, charts and graphs into a Word file to create a report.

Plenary
Having now completed the full cycle of developing and reporting by using a spreadsheet model, pupils can give their opinions as to the effectiveness of using a model in comparison to carrying out the work in other ways. A class discussion can centre on the use of an electronic formatted model being quicker and easier to use than a manual version. Pupils could create a diary of events for how they have developed and used the Sponsor Scheme model.

Differentiation
Most pupils will be able to select and create the correct format of graphs to show data clearly, but it may not always be the most suitable and pupils may need assistance in understanding why they have chosen the selected format over others. More able pupils will choose an appropriate format, will be able to make reasoned judgements for their selection and will be able to handle updating data and the implications that the process could have for the documents they are creating.

Suggested starters

1 Whole class discussion. Select pupils to come out and draw some tables, charts and graphs on the whiteboard. Label their drawings with the following: pie chart, column chart, line graph, data table (add any missed by pupils). Ask them to give

you a situation where each of the examples could be used and where they would not be suitable. The purpose of the discussion is to test the level of knowledge that pupils have about different information formats. (They should be able to identify the use of pie charts with percentages and that column charts are suitable for a young audience.)

2   Pupils to work in groups of four/five. Explain to the whole class that they are going to be working with graphs and charts. Create a series of labels: pie chart, column chart, data table and line graph. Hand the labels out to the groups and allow no more than five minutes for pupils to write an accurate definition – no drawings-only answers. They should add an example of its use. Select pupils to read out their definitions and ask the class to comment on how they could be improved. At the end you should have a definitive class definition for each type of graph/chart.

3   Whole class discussion. Work out a series of five questions that the pupils can respond to quickly, for example:

● How many like tea?
● How many can paddle a canoe?
● How many have got one sister?
● How many have got two sisters?
● How many have got three dogs?

Ask the class for a show of hands as a response to each question. Create a tally chart on the whiteboard with one mark for every two responses. After you have done the full series of questions, ask the pupils what the questions were and what the tally marks represent. The purpose of the activity is to demonstrate how important it is to provide clear information and record and label data. The tally chart could be misinterpreted and the questions could be anything. Ask them if there are other means of presenting the information so that it is easy to understand.

Notes on Tasks

Task 1 (Green)

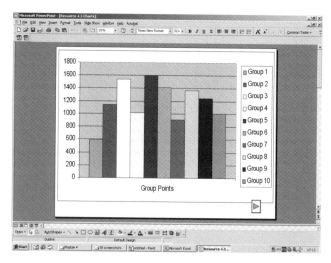

Pupils work out which type of chart or graph they should use to present the Sponsor Scheme information in report. They look at **Resource 4.5 Charts** which shows four different methods of displaying the same data. They make notes about which is the clearest form and from which they found it easiest to answer questions.

Task 2 (Green)

Pupils create a series of different charts and graphs from the last saved version of their Sponsors Scheme file. They save three of the charts/graphs as separate worksheets in the file, the fourth they save in the worksheet where the data has been taken. They comment upon which they think shows the data clearly and which one they would choose to use to illustrate different situations.

A demonstration of creating each type of chart/graph (through a large monitor or data projector) could be carried out. See Skills help on pages 107–108 of the Pupil Book.

Module Task

Ensure pupils have carried out Task 2 before beginning the Module Task, where they prepare a report for the sponsors. Less able pupils may need some guidance as to the size of text boxes to use, or where to place the different items. Pupils discuss and compare their report with a partner. They decide any areas they would want to improve/change.

A demonstration of copying and pasting from an original document into a report (through a large monitor or data projector) could be carried out. See Skills help on page 110 of the Pupil Book.

Task 3 (Red)

Pupils working at the higher level are asked to change some data within Week 1 of the Sponsor Scheme model. They produce a new chart to show the different data. They copy this chart alongside the version in the Module Task report, and save this as a new report to show the comparison between the two sets of information.

Task 4 (Green)

Pupils have completed a full modelling process from developing the spreadsheet model to producing a report. They give their opinions as to the effectiveness of using a model in comparison to working in other ways. They discuss the use of an electronic formatted model and whether it is quicker and easier to use than a manual version.

Homework suggestion

Pupils could complete Task 4, then, in the next lesson, participate in a class discussion on whether the use of an electronic formatted model is really quicker and easier to use than a manual version.

Suggested extension activity

As an additional activity pupils could:

1   Load a presentation program such as PowerPoint.

2   Open a new show.

3   Open the last saved version of their Sponsor Scheme report containing the charts and graphs.

4   Select one of the charts and copy it.

5   Paste it into the presentation slide show and investigate different ways of animating the slide to show the data to an audience.

6   Save this presentation in the shared area.

Level guide

Level 5

Pupils working at Level 5 and above will be able to create graphs and charts that show the data clearly. They will choose an appropriate format and will be able to make reasoned judgements for their selection. They will copy and paste the data confidently between the two documents, being able to adjust the size and placement of images to match the required layout. They will be able to handle updating data and the implications that the process could have for the documents they are creating. They will be able to discriminate between when it is best to use electronic models and when it is better to carry out calculations manually.

Level 4

Pupils working at Level 4 will be able to select and create the correct format of graphs to show data clearly. The format will not always be the most suitable and pupils will not always know why they have chosen the selected format over others. They will be able to copy graphs and charts between documents and rearrange them to make them match the desired layout. They will be able to understand the strengths of using a model over other methods but will not always be sure when not to use an electronic format.

Level 3

Pupils working at Level 3 and below will create charts and graphs that show the data but they may not always choose the most appropriate format. They will be able to copy and paste the items between the documents with assistance. They will be able to discuss the strengths of using a spreadsheet model over other forms of modelling but will not be able to discriminate as to when not to use an electronic format.

Module 4
Community playground

To complete Module 4 pupils are required to set up a spreadsheet model to investigate the cost of building a community playground.

Resources

Pupil Book: Module 4, pages 78–110

Module 4 Assignment Evaluation form

Spreadsheet and word processing software

National Curriculum Level indicators based upon pupil outcome

Level indicators At the end of this assignment		
Pupils working at Level 3 will: • Put the data supplied into a basic spreadsheet model of the initial cost for the playground • With help, use formulas to calculate totals • Make limited use of the model to see the effects of changing the value of variables • Produce a simple e-report based upon the data in the spreadsheet	Pupils working at Level 4 will: • Use the data supplied to create a spreadsheet model that could be used to predict the potential cost for the playgroup • Use formulas to carry out the necessary calculations and make changes to variables • Check the accuracy of the information in their model • Produce graphs and charts and copy data from their spreadsheet into a report and combine with text	Pupils working at Level 5 will: • Use the data provided to set up a spreadsheet model that is efficiently laid out and functions effectively • Refine formulas to enable the model to answer 'What if … ?' questions • Check the accuracy of the model by asking others to check it • Demonstrate an understanding of the use of absolute cell references • Create appropriate forms of displaying data for inclusion in a report

Module 5
Data handling

Where this module fits in	Prior learning
This module builds on: Work done in KS2 POS, particularly the 'Finding things out' and 'Developing ideas and making things happen' sections. Also Module 2 'Using data and information sources' and Module 4 'Modelling and presenting numeric data'.	To make good progress, pupils starting this module need to be able to: 1 Gather information from a variety of sources 2 Know basic database terminology such as records, fields, tables 3 Describe some of the data types used in databases (alphanumeric, numeric) 4 Understand what questionnaires are used for 5 Create simple graphs and charts (pie, column, line graphs)
The main concept of this module is: To find out how to collect relevant information to be able to answer questions; to be able to create a file designed to handle data and to use database functions to interrogate data and consider the plausibility of the conclusions drawn.	
This module leads on to: Modules on data handling in Student Books 2 and 3.	Revision of these areas is in Module 5 Prior learning.

Subject knowledge needed by teachers

To teach this module you will need to know how to:	Information on this aspect can be found in:
Load and save work in a shared area	Pupil Book pages 1, 24
Use presentation, word processing and spreadsheet software	Pupil Book pages 24–31, 48, 103–110
Use the Internet to find information and download it	Pupil Book pages 32, 38–41, 49
Use data handling software and create data files	Pupil Book pages 111–112, 125, 136–137 Resource 5.4 Data in
Sort and make selective searches of data in a data file	Pupil Book pages 112, 129–130, 137 Resource 5.4 Data in
Produce a range of graphs and charts from data files	Pupil Book pages 107–108
Explain the difference between various data types including alphanumeric and numeric data	Pupil Book pages 112, 125

Level indicators
At the end of this module

Pupils working at Level 3 will:	Pupils working at Level 4 will:	Pupils working at Level 5 will:
• Find and use appropriate stored information, following straightforward lines of enquiry • Generate, develop and organise their work • Share and exchange their ideas with others	• Find and interrogate information, understanding the need for care in framing questions • Interpret their findings, question plausibility and recognise poor quality information leads to unreliable results	• Select the information that they need for different purposes • Check the accuracy of data and organise it in a form suitable for processing • Critically evaluate the fitness for purpose of their work as it progresses

Overview of module content and how it fits with the DfES sample teaching units			
Module in Pupil Book	Matches DfES lesson (in terms of content and and teaching objectives covered)	Outline of content	Progress on module task
Module 5 Prior learning PB pages 111–112			
5.1 Looking at data PB pages 113–116 TB pages 98–100	Lesson 7.5.1	Knowledge about a database and the structure of data files. Reliability of data. Use data handling software to organise and derive new information.	Retrieve information from a prepared data file. Create simple graphs from data.
5.2 Presenting information PB pages 117–119 TB pages 101–103	Lesson 7.5.2	Understand what a hypothesis is and how one can be tested. Use percentages to help interpret data.	Convert data into percentages.
5.3 Creating a questionnaire PB pages 120–123 TB pages 104–106	Lesson 7.5.3	Look at the way questions have to be phrased to gain accurate information that will be valid to test a hypothesis. Understand how to record responses when formulating a questionnaire. Selecting a valid sample.	Setting up a questionnaire that consists of relevant questions.
5.4 Creating a data handling file PB pages 124–126 TB pages 107–109	Lesson 7.5.4	Classifying the responses to a questionnaire so that data can be entered into a data file in a meaningful way. Creating a data-handling file so that the responses can be interrogated.	Working out the layout for a data file that will hold the responses from the questionnaires. Ensuring that the responses will be valid.
5.5 Entering, checking and testing data PB pages 127–131 TB pages 110–112	Lesson 7.5.5	Data entry. Use of a data file to answer questions and test hypothesis. Understand ways that errors can be found and trapped in data files. Setting questions for others to answer using a data file.	Enter data into data handling files. Carry out queries on the data to gather evidence to test hypothesis.
5.6 Drawing conclusions from data PB pages 132–134 TB pages 113–115	Lesson 7.5.6	Draw conclusions from data. Create a report to show that a hypothesis is found to be true or not valid. Copy and paste data and charts between a data file and a word processing document.	Draw conclusions and produce a report containing evidence from the data to support them.
Module 5 Assignment PB page 135 TB page 116	All of 7.5	Assignment covering the same learning objectives as those covered in Module 5 lessons, but in the context of the hypothesis that '12-year-old girls get more pocket money than 12-year-old boys do'. Scope for pupils to perform at Levels 3, 4 and 5.	

Cross curricular opportunities	
Subject	Programme of study section
Maths 2 (number and algebra)	6g (working with graphs)
Maths 3 (handling data)	All of this section relates closely to Module 5
	2d–e (collecting data in fieldwork)
	2g (data logging)
	2i–j (presenting data as graphs and charts)
	2k–l (creating and testing hypotheses)
Science 2 (life processes)	2a (recording and analysing information about diets)
	3a (recording and analysing results of experiments on photosynthesis)
	4n (recording and analysing bacteria population)
	5f (recording and analysing toxin levels in a food chain)
Science 3 (materials)	1a (classifying materials)
Design and Technology	4b (analyse materials and properties)
Geography	1c (collect and present statistical evidence)
	1d (analyse data)
	1f and 2f (communicate information derived from data)
	6j (collect and analyse data on transport and the environment)

Unit 5.1
Looking at data

In this unit pupils look at some information from a database. They consider the reliability of the data and learn how charts and graphs can help them understand data.

Supports DfES sample teaching unit 7.5.1

ICT Framework Objectives

FINDING THINGS OUT

Using data and information sources
- Identify the purpose of an information source and whether it is likely to be biased.
- Understand how someone using an information source could be misled by missing or inaccurate information.

Organising and investigating
- In an investigation:
  - use software to represent data in simple graphs, charts or tables, justifying the choice of representation
  - derive new information from data.

Key vocabulary

accurate, bar chart, bias, data, database, download, field, Internet, information source, interrogate, numeric data, origin, pie chart, reliable, table, uniform resource locator (URL), value

Resources

Pupil Book: Module 5 Unit 5.1, pages 113–116
Resource 5.1 Numbers
Resource 5.1 Population
Software for data handling and word processing
Access to the Internet

Suggested lesson plan

Starter
The Starters involve class discussions about the use of databases and make a suitable introduction to the nature of databases. Pupils have the opportunity to do manually what a database program would do automatically.

Main part
As a class introduction to using data, pupils can carry out Task 1 as a whole class activity. They are presented with a set of data taken from a large world population database and asked to interpret the data and speculate how it could be used. The Module Task expands the interrogation of data to find out more information. Pupils will need to be able to understand symbols used as operators and to consider what the information they are finding really means. They are encouraged to visit the source website for the information and to judge whether the data is valid. Pupils working at the higher level will be asked to identify possible reasons for population distributions in Task 2. In Task 3 pupils are asked to produce a chart and a graph from a data set.

Plenary
Prior to setting the homework, have a class discussion about the way that graphs are used to provide information, for example in television news programmes.

Differentiation
Most pupils will understand that databases can store large amounts of data and that the data can be searched and sorted. Some will need assistance to create graphs and charts from a data set but more able pupils can be asked to find specific information from a data set and to discuss what the data might mean. They can create graphs and charts representing the data and may be able to make a reasoned decision about the use of the graphs and charts to display the data.

Suggested starters

1 Whole class activity. The purpose of this activity is to develop an awareness of why databases are used. Ask pupils to write down as many first names as they can think of in two minutes. Go around the class making a list of all of the names the pupils have thought of. Add in the duplicate names. When the list reaches 30 plus, stop and find all of the names that appear more than once. Discuss how a database could do the same task in moments, plus how it could interrogate much larger samples. Add in the other types of sorts and searches that database software is capable of.

2 Split the class into groups of four/five. Ask each group to come up with a list of all the stationery items that a typical office suppliers would stock. Allow not more than five minutes. Ask the pupils to put their list into alphabetical order and then to make a separate list of all of the items beginning with the letter 'P'. This will enable them to experience the type of work that a database can do. When the pupils have all sorted and listed their products, ask them to split them into categories. They need to work out what the categories are first and then to split them up. This starts to build knowledge about fields and field names. Compile a list of the categories on a whiteboard and list all of the items. Explain how this would form a database with fields and records.

3 Whole class discussion. Ask the pupils where they think databases are used. Write a list on a whiteboard or create a list on a computer displayed through a data projector or large monitor. Prompt as necessary by adding in some that they might not come up with, for example DVLA, hospital record office. When the list contains 10 plus places, discuss the nature of the records that would be stored – personal, sensitive, confidential, top security. Ask them how many times they think one person's details might be stored on different systems. The purpose of this activity is to raise pupils' awareness of the power of databases and information. Ask them if they know about the Data Protection Act and what it is for.

Notes on Tasks

Task 1 (Green)

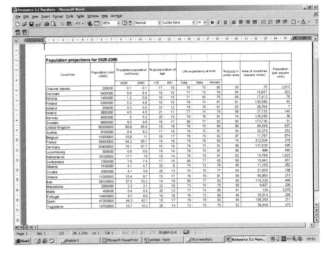

Pupils use **Resource 5.1 Numbers**, which contains data from a global population projection database created by an American university. The data is presented as numerical measurements and the pupils have to spot what the actual numbers mean. There are arithmetical operators shown; some pupils might need assistance in understanding the symbols. Make a list of the things that they suggest could be extracted from this data set, for example which country has the largest population.

Module Task

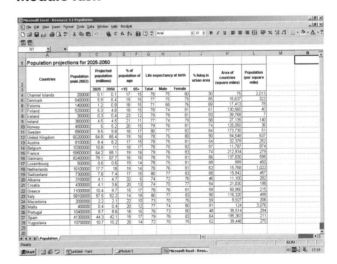

In the Module Task pupils work with a partner to interrogate the data to answer several questions. Allow pupils to attempt questions 1–4 of the task using just the Word file (**Resource 5.1 Numbers**). Then introduce **Resource 5.1 Population**, which is the same data in an Excel file, and encourage the pupils to use the **sort** function and redo questions 1–4. Discuss how this makes the task easier. Some questions, for example the second part of question 5, require pupils to perfom a calculation to get the answer. Pupils should continue to use **Resource 5.1 Population** for questions 5–6. They access the URL of a website with population data by going to http://www.heinemann.co.uk/hotlinks and look at the statistics online. They have to decide whether this is an official website and therefore whether the data on it can be trusted. The website could be set as a favourite in the pupils' area on the school network.

Task 2 (Red)

Pupils working at the higher level look at the data set to identify trends in the population. They also try to work out why the statistics might show the figures that they do for places like Malta and the Channel Islands (high population per square mile because they are islands).

Task 3 (Green)

Pupils produce a chart and a graph from the data set in **Resource 5.1 Population**. It might be necessary to review how charts and graphs are produced in a spreadsheet file, or pupils could be referred to Skills help on pages 107–108 of the Pupil Book. Pupils compare the graph and the chart for ease of reading and understanding what the data means. This task is similar to ones in Module 4. You should emphasise that charts and graphs are also very useful tools for analysing large data sets.

Task 4 (Green)

To end the first unit pupils collect samples of graphs and charts as shown in newspapers, magazines or downloaded from the Internet. They make notes about what the graphs/charts represent and how they were being used.

Homework suggestion

Pupils could do Task 4.

Suggested extension activity

As an additional activity pupils could:

1 Look at **Resource 5.1 Numbers**.

2 List five ways that they think companies or organisations could make use of this data, for example one idea could be that a company making vitamin pills for the elderly might choose to publicise their products in Italy and Switzerland, as the life expectancy is high there.

3 Select one of their ideas and show from the data set how they could make use of it.

Level guide

Level 5

Pupils working at Level 5 and above will be able to identify advantages in using a database to store, interrogate and retrieve large amounts of data for specific purposes. They will be able to interrogate a data set to find specified data efficiently. They will identify trends and speculate as to what information underlies the stored data. They will make a reasoned decision about the use of graphs or charts to display data.

Level 4

Pupils working at Level 4 will be able to understand the need for having databases to store, interrogate and retrieve data. They will be able to find specific information from a data set and discuss what the data might mean. They will be able to create graphs and charts representing the data from a data set.

Level 3

Pupils working at Level 3 and below will understand that databases can store large amounts of data and that the data can be searched and sorted. They will work with assistance to find data from a set of data and create graphs and charts from a data set.

Unit 5.2
Presenting information

In this unit pupils learn how to use data to draw conclusions and how to present data in different formats, such as percentages and graphs.

Supports DfES sample teaching unit 7.5.2

ICT Framework Objectives

FINDING THINGS OUT

Organising and investigating

- *In an investigation:*
  - *use an appropriate data handling structure to answer questions and draw conclusions*
  - *use software to represent data in simple graphs, charts or tables, justifying the choice of representation*
  - *check whether conclusions are plausible.*

Key vocabulary

data type, hypothesis, plausible, viewpoint

Suggested lesson plan

Starter

The Starter activities introduce pupils to the concept of a hypothesis. They have the opportunity to look at different forms of data and deduce whether it supports a stated hypothesis or not.

Main part

In Task 1 pupils are asked to think of a hypothesis that could be easily tested. They use the class as the subject for the hypothesis. They examine a data set and provide notes on how they would use the data set to test their hypothesis. The Module Task takes this one stage further and pupils examine two data sets that show the same data in different formats, one as raw numerical data and the other as a percentage. They determine how the percentages have been derived from the numerical data.

Resources

Pupil Book: Module 5 Unit 5.2, pages 117–119
Resource 5.2 Collection
Resource 5.2 Prove it!
Resource 5.2 Weather data
Large computer screen display
Software for data handling and word processing
Collection of graphs from different sources, e.g. newspapers, magazines and downloaded from the Internet

Plenary

As an introduction to their homework, hold a whole class discussion about the way the data was presented to them in this lesson and ask them to consider the length of time that was necessary to collect the data that they have been using. Lead into the way that the data was collected, then in Task 4 pupils work out how they can collect data for a data file that they will create. The subject has to be about holidays.

Differentiation

Most pupils will understand how to test a hypothesis and will be able to find information from a data set to test a hypothesis. More able pupils can be asked to examine data to see what hypotheses could be tested from it. They will appreciate the difference in presenting data in different formats and can use a prepared spreadsheet file to generate percentages.

Suggested starters

1 Whole class discussion. Ask pupils if they have heard of the word hypothesis. Do they know what it is? Write on a whiteboard or display on a monitor the following:

a Most men like black cats

b Women buy more shampoo than men

c More people stay at home for their holidays than go abroad

Ask the class if they think these are true or not. Choose pupils to give their reasons why they think they are true or not. Ask them how they could prove it. This discussion will lead on to understanding what a hypothesis is and how it could be tested.

2 Split the class into groups of four/five. Provide each group with a different hypothesis written on cards. Also provide them with a series of charts or graphs that come from data supporting the hypotheses. Make sure that groups get different charts and hypotheses. Ask a member of each group to read out the hypothesis. Group members then look at the graph/chart that they have and decide whether theirs is the one that shows accurately the data that could support the hypothesis.

Notes on Tasks

Task 1 (Green)

Pupils are asked to write down a hypothesis about members of the class. They should be encouraged to consider ones that could be easily tested, for example more boys have blonde hair than girls. Discuss methods that could be used to test out several of their suggestions. Draw on ideas such as counting the numbers of people with blonde hair, and what groups they would need to consider (boys/girls, blonde/not blonde).

Task 2 (Green)

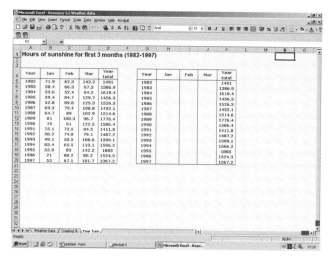

Pupils work with a partner to think of a hypothesis that they could test from the data provided. **Resource 5.2 Weather data** is a data table taken from a weather station in the UK. It shows the monthly totals for rainfall and sunshine from 1982–1997. Pupils record their hypotheses on the worksheet **Resource 5.2 Prove it!** and make notes on how they think it could be tested.

Task 3 (Red)

Pupils working at the higher level work individually to refine their hypotheses by adding another level of complexity. Each pupil records a second version of their hypothesis on the **Resource 5.2 Prove it!** and gives it to a partner to test out. The partner first declares whether they think it is plausible and then goes on to try and test it out.

Module Task

In the Module Task pupils use **Resource 5.2 Weather data** to find out how to present data as a percentage. This is largely a skills-based task, but you should emphasise the reasons for converting the numbers to percentages, i.e. it is easier to compare them than when they are simple totals. The 'Creating percentages' worksheet has been formatted as percentages. Pupils should click on the cells in the right hand table to understand how it is performed. When they are confident that they understand the principle, they should go to worksheet 'Your turn' within **Resource 5.2 Weather data** and create their own percentage formula. Remind them to use copy and fill.

Task 4 (Green)

To start to build experience in collecting information, pupils collect information about holidays from a range of people. The worksheet, **Resource 5.2 Collection** provides a structure for them to record information that they collect.
If appropriate, pupils could be asked to create their own collection forms using word processing software. The collection of the information could be set as homework to ensure a range of different people can be asked.

Homework suggestion

Pupils could do Task 4.

Suggested extension activity

As an additional activity pupils could:

1   Look at **Resource 5.2 Weather data**.

2   Enter formulas to calculate the sunshine totals for Spring, Summer, Autumn and Winter. Hint: Spring is March, April and May.

3   Copy and fill in their formulas for all years.

4   Starting in field T23, enter the same quarterly sunshine information as percentages of the total, for each year and each quarter.

Level guide

Level 5

Pupils working at Level 5 and above will be able to create a hypothesis that could be tested. They will be able to analyse data to see what could be extracted from it and the hypotheses that could be supported by the data. They will be able to work with data to create a percentage in a spreadsheet and understand that when data is presented as percentages it can be compared more easily with other data. They will be able to discuss the type of questions that should be asked to acquire specific information and will be able to identify a suitable sample.

Level 4

Pupils working at Level 4 will understand what a hypothesis is and how it could be tested. They will be able to create a hypothesis but will be unsure what they would need to do to test it. They will be able to examine data to see what hypotheses could be tested from it. They will appreciate the difference in presenting data in different formats and will be able to use a prepared spreadsheet file to generate percentages. They will be able to discuss the types of questions that could be used to gain information from a specific range of people, although some of the questions will not be focused.

Level 3

Pupils working at Level 3 and below will understand how to test a hypothesis and, with help, will be able to create one. They will be able to find information from a data set to test a hypothesis, but will have trouble in deciding what information they really need to support it. They will make use of a prepared spreadsheet to examine data presented as percentages. They will be able to create questions about holidays but will not identify a suitable sample.

Unit 5.3
Creating a questionnaire

In this unit pupils design a questionnaire which will collect relevant data in a suitable format so that they can test a hypothesis.

Supports DfES sample teaching unit 7.5.3

ICT Framework Objectives

FINDING THINGS OUT

Using data and information sources
● Identify what information is relevant to a task.

Organising and investigating
● In an investigation:
  – design a questionnaire or data collection sheet to provide relevant data
  – check whether conclusions are plausible.

Key vocabulary

alphanumeric, data type, numeric, questionnaire, sample, sample composition, sample size

Resources

Pupil Book: Module 5 Unit 5.3, pages 120–123
Resource 5.3 Questionnaire
Resource 2.1 Questions – (from earlier Unit)
Large computer screen display
Software for data handling and word processing

Suggested lesson plan

Starter
The Starter activities emphasise that the information obtained in a survey is only as good as the questionnaire devised to obtain the information. Pupils get experience in phrasing questions in an appropriate way and an introduction to the different methods of questioning.

Main part
In Task 1 pupils look at data they collected and create a hypothesis based upon the questionnaire they devised. They take this a step further in Task 2 and start to plan out the questions that they could use to test a given hypothesis. The Module Task builds on the previous tasks to make the pupils look at how they might ask a sample group questions that will test the hypothesis. They create a spreadsheet file as a questionnaire that will be used to record the responses from their sample group. The pupils will need to understand how the data needs to be used to generate meaningful results.

Plenary
As a follow on from Task 1, where pupils have looked at the data that they have expanded as an individual, as a pair and as a group, a class discussion would be appropriate to pull ideas together. It can be based on the case study on page 123 of the Pupil Book and should show how locally based data can differ from the national picture.

Differentiation
Most pupils will be able to set up a spreadsheet file as a questionnaire but will need practice in formulating the questions, formatting and editing the file. Some guidance for all pupils might be required when selecting a sample for questioning that will provide valid responses.

Suggested starters

1 Whole class discussion. Pupils need to be aware that the information that they get as responses to questions will be dependent upon the way that they ask the questions. Tell pupils that you want to be able to find out what the most popular drink is that is sold in the school canteen. Ask pupils what sources of information should be used and what questions could be used to find out relevant information.

2 Paired activity. Pupils make a list of five closed questions that could be asked to find out about somebody's interests. They then write a second list of five open-ended questions that could be asked about the same subject. For each set of questions they decide what type of responses they would get and how the information could be used. The purpose is to remind pupils about the different methods of questioning and how important it is to phrase questions in the correct way.

3 Whole class discussion. Ask pupils what type of questions they should ask to get YES or NO answers. Tell them that they have to get directions from a partner that would help them get to their partner's grandparents' house (it doesn't matter where the grandparents live for this activity – near or abroad). The only restriction is that their partner can only answer YES or NO to questions. Allow the pupils five minutes to get the directions. Review the process of asking the questions and ask them to identify any problems that arose.

Notes on Tasks

Task 1 (Green)

Pupils work with a partner to look at the data that they both collected in Task 4 of Unit 5.2. They examine it to see if they can come up with a hypothesis that could be supported by the data. When they have formulated a hypothesis they ask a wider group of pupils to see if the data that they collected would be appropriate to support their hypothesis and they also look to see if their data supports the other hypothesis. From this level they go on to work out a set of questions could be used to gain data nationally.

Task 2 (Green)

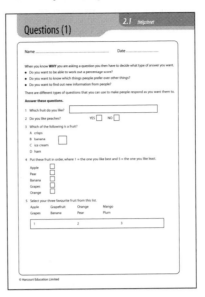

After exploring how hypotheses can be drawn out from data, pupils are provided with a hypothesis that they will work with over the remaining units in Module 5. The hypothesis that they will test is '12-year-olds have more foreign holidays today than they would have had in the 1970s'. In order to do this, pupils will be creating a questionnaire to collect data. This would be a good point to revise work done in Module 2 on creating questionnaires. They could be given copies of the Helpsheet, **Resource 2.1 Questions** to help them with this task.

They access the worksheet, **Resource 5.3 Questionnaire** and plan out the questions that they think are needed to gain relevant information.

As a test, they also have to add the type of responses that they think they would get from the questions. They will need time to reflect and to establish that their questions will actually provide valid responses.

Task 3 (Red)

Pupils working at the higher level can be asked to work out the data type that they are expecting in the responses, i.e. alphanumeric, numeric, text. They can be encouraged to use a code for the answers A, N or T. Although not needed at this stage, the use of coding like this will take them further on with database development work in the future.

Module Task

Pupils are to create a data collection form or questionnaire. This is not the same thing as the data handling file which is used to share and analyse the responses to the questionnaire. That will be created in Unit 5.4. In the worked example in **Resource 5.4 Data in**, both the questionnaire and the data handling file are created as different worksheets in the same spreadsheet file, but this is not essential: the questionnaire could be created in word processing software if preferred. The important thing for pupils to remember is that the responses to their questionnaire must be easy to process by a computer and be capable of classifying respondents in ways which will be useful to test the hypothesis. It is likely that all but the most able pupils will need some support with this task.

Task 4 (Green)

Before tackling this task, pupils should be reminded about how to select a valid sample (see Unit 2.1). Task 4 could be done as a class activity to get pupils to think about the people that they need to ask to gain information that will help them to test the hypothesis. The outcome of the task should be an agreed list of people from whom each pupil will collect responses, e.g. three people younger than me, three people the same age, my parents/ grandparents.

Homework suggestion

Pupils collect data from the people agreed as the sample in Task 4. Responses are recorded on a printout of the worksheet, **Resource 5.3 Questionnaire**.

Suggested extension activity

As an additional activity pupils could:

1   Consider how big they think the sample should be in order to be sure that the responses really will prove their hypothesis.

2   See what they can find out about sampling and sample sizes used in market research.

Level guide

Level 5

Pupils working at Level 5 and above will be able to formulate questions that are relevant to a task. They will be able to identify the different data types that they will receive as responses and code their questions to match the data type. They will be able to set up a questionnaire in a spreadsheet and work out how they can generate meaningful results from the responses that they receive. They will be able to select an appropriate sample group for questioning.

Level 4

Pupils working at Level 4 will formulate questions that are sensible and that will provide relevant information. They will create a spreadsheet file as a questionnaire and discuss how they might set it up to generate data that can be used to test the hypothesis. They will select a sample for questioning that will provide valid responses although they may include some people who are not valid within the sample.

Level 3

Pupils working at Level 3 and below will work with assistance to create a series of questions that can be used to test the hypothesis. They will set up a spreadsheet file as a questionnaire but will need help in the formatting and editing of the file. They will need to be guided as to the most appropriate sample to use to gather data.

Unit 5.4

Creating a data handling file

In this unit pupils learn how to refine their methods of questioning and design a data handling file to enable them to test a hypothesis.

Supports DfES sample teaching unit 7.5.4

ICT Framework Objectives

FINDING THINGS OUT

Organising and investigating

● In an investigation:
  – design an appropriate data handling structure
  – design a questionnaire to provide relevant data.

Key vocabulary

classify, data structure, field, numeric, questionnaire, sort, value

Suggested lesson plan

Starter

The Starter activities give pupils the opportunity to understand how to begin to code data they receive from questionnaires in preparation for a data handling file. They learn to code responses and look at the different ways data can be entered into a database.

Main part

In Task 1 pupils look at the suggested questions and compare them to ones that they have used so far. It is essential that the pupils can understand the importance of making the questions very precise and relevant to the task. They change their original questions to ones that are agreed as a whole class. This provides a consistent measure for data input.
The Module Task provides the opportunity for pupils to create their own version of a data handling file. Pupils who have problems creating their own can customise a file provided on the CD ROM to match their needs.

Resources

Pupil Book: Module 5 Unit 5.4, pages 124–126
Resource 5.4 Data in
Large computer screen display
Software for data handling and word processing

Plenary

Bring together the work on questionnaires by doing Task 3. Here pupils are asked to consider how easily they can enter data into their own data handling file and whether they will be able to interrogate it to classify their results.

Differentiation

Most pupils will be able to enter questions into a prepared data handling file. They will be able to discuss the way the data will be entered and evaluate the layout. The challenge will come in rewording the questions to make them more specific to the task, editing the data handling file to suit their own style, and evaluating the data handling file in terms of ease of inputting data.

Suggested starters

1   Whole class discussion. Pupils need to understand how to set up coding for the data when they create a data file. Ask them how many have completed a quiz in a magazine (normally to find out if they are lucky or something similar). Ask them to explain how the scoring often works,

for example: If you answered mainly a's you are... . Explain that this is one way that they could code the responses that they get back from their questionnaires.

2. Whole class activity. Hand out a customer service evaluation form from a restaurant/hotel. Ask pupils what they think about the questions. Ask them to try to work out how the company will be able to judge customer satisfaction over a day, a week or a year. The objective is to make them look at the ways that the data could be entered into a database and analysed at different times.

3. Whole class discussion. Tell pupils that you would like to test the hypothesis that 'Most pupils watch television for at least four hours each night'.
Ask them to select the questions from a list displayed on the whiteboard or large monitor that would be sensible questions to ask. Ask them to explain why they are rejecting some of the questions. The questions could include:

- Do you watch television?

- Do you watch it each night?

- Which programmes do you watch? (rejected)

- Do you like *Coronation Street*? (rejected)

- Do you watch it for more than three hours at a time?

- Do you watch it for less than five hours? (rejected)

Notes on Tasks

Task 1 (Green)

Before they tackle this task, explain to pupils that researchers often test and refine questionnaires many times before finally using them for real.

The outcome of this task should be a final set of questions and possible answers agreed upon by the whole class. Pupils can start the work of refining in pairs, but after a few minutes, ask one of the more able pupils to show their questionnaire as a starting point. Take suggestions for improvement from the rest of the class to make sure that the class understands why certain suggestions are

accepted and others are not. Leave the final agreed version up on the display. You will also need to print it off and make enough copies for each pupil to have a copy. Each pupil will also keep a copy of the final version of their own questionnaire for their portfolio.

Task 2 (Red)

Pupils working at the higher level are introduced to an extended hypothesis. They are asked to work out what difference it will make to their questionnaire if the hypothesis changes to '12-year-olds have more **and longer** foreign holidays than they would have done in the 1970s.'

Module Task

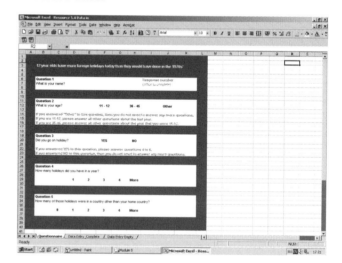

Pupils are to create a data handling file to store the responses to the questionnaire. Where possible they should be allowed to create their own version. However, there is a worked example of the file that can be used by pupils who find the setting up of the file difficult. The file, **Resource 5.4 Data in**, contains three worksheets, the first is the questionnaire, the second is a sample as though responses have been received and the third is an empty response form.

Give out a copy of the final, class-agreed version of the questionnaire. Each pupil completes it using the data which they gathered in Task 4, Unit 5.3.

Task 3 (Green)

Pupils evaluate how easy it will be to enter the data from the questionnaire into their data handling file and how easily they will be able to classify the data that comes back.

Homework suggestion

Pupils could undertake Task 3.

Suggested extension activity

As an additional activity pupils could:

1 Load the latest version of their data handling file.

2 Look at the way that the file has been set up.

3 Think of a change that could be made to the method of inputting data to improve accuracy, for example, drop-down lists.

4 Find out how to make these improvements using the software provided.

Level guide

Level 5

Pupils working at Level 5 and above will be able to refine their questions to make them more precise and suitable for the task. They will be able to create an original data handling file that will be capable of generating realistic and valid results. They will be able to evaluate critically the layout of their data handling file in terms of ease of input and classifying data.

Level 4

Pupils working at Level 4 will reword questions to make them more specific to the task. They will edit a prepared data handling file to suit their own style. They will evaluate the layout of the data handling file in terms of appearance and ease of inputting data.

Level 3

Pupils working at Level 3 and below will use prepared questions and enter them into a prepared data handling file. They will be able to discuss the way the data will be entered into the file and evaluate the layout of the file.

In this unit pupils learn how to enter data and use charts and graphs to check the accuracy of the data. They also learn how to sort and search data.

Supports DfES sample teaching unit 7.5.5

ICT Framework Objectives

FINDING THINGS OUT

Searching and selecting
- *Narrow down a search to achieve more relevant results.*

Organising and investigating
- *In an investigation:*
  - *check data efficiently for errors*
  - *investigate relationships between variables*
  - *use software to represent data in simple graphs, charts or tables, justifying the choice of representation.*

Suggested lesson plan

Starter
The objective of the Starters is to raise pupils' awareness of the methods of spotting errors.

Main part
Task 1 provides pupils with a resource file of a set of data that contains several errors. It gives them the opportunity to spot the errors and consider any precautions that could be taken or procedures to stop the errors happening. In Task 2 pupils are encouraged to work out a way to speed up data entry and to make frequent saves of their work to avoid loss of data if they make mistakes. Once completed, they can check for errors again. Task 3 introduces **Sort** and **Filter** options as a means of checking data. The Module Task brings all these techniques together in one exercise. Pupils working at the higher level will be carrying out more complex filtered searches in Task 4 to find the answers to additional questions.

Key vocabulary
effectively, efficiently, enquiry, improve, numeric, revise, sort, variable

Resources
Pupil Book: Module 5 Unit 5.5, pages 127–131
Resource 5.4 Data in
Resource 5.5 Errors
Resource 5.5 Trails
Large computer screen display
Software for data handling and word processing

Plenary
You can suggest that pupils carry out additional work on interrogating their data files by using their own instead of the prepared file. They set a series of questions that they and a partner find the answers to. They compare their results and consider any additional data needed to improve accuracy.

Suggested starters

1   Whole class discussion. Ask the pupils if they can tell you ways that errors like the three examples here can be found before documents are shown in public.

They went fro a long walk (proofreading as fro would not be found by spellchecker)

They each had there coat with them (grammar check by computer or proofreading)

They each hud an ice cream (spellcheck)

The objective is to raise pupils' awareness of the methods of spotting errors.

2 Whole class discussion. Pupils may not be aware of the different format for dates used in other countries. Ask them what day this is: 03/11/03.

Answers you might receive include: 3rd November or 11th March. Ask pupils what they would need to know to make sure that this type of error did not happen in their data files.

3 Whole class discussion. Ask the pupils how many mistakes they can spot in this passage of text:

'The pupils had just come back from their long summer holiday on 5th Febraury. They would be preparing for there tests that were to take place at the end of the month beginning on the 30th. They shuld all have completed a Unite of work based upon Christmas in the sun.'

(Mistakes are:

Pupils live in Australia so it is their summer

Spelling of February

Should be 'their' not 'there'

No 30th of February

Spelling of 'should'

Unit not 'Unite')

Ask them to explain how these could be corrected.

Notes on Tasks

Task 1 (Green)

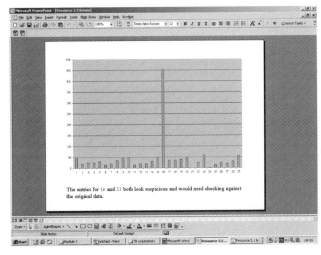

Pupils use **Resource 5.5 Trails** which shows data from a wildlife park in the UK. They identify where they think there are errors in the text and discuss their findings with a partner. They work out if there is any method of preventing the errors. Pupils working at the higher level could be introduced to the idea of validation and verification of data.

Task 2 (Green)

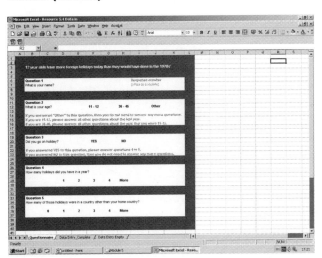

Pupils work with a partner to enter data from the questionnaire into the data handling files that they created in Unit 5.4. They use **Resource 5.5 Errors** to see how effective it can be to set up a column chart to locate potential errors. They create a column chart of their data as a check on accuracy of data entry.

Task 3 (Green)

Pupils interrogate a prepared data file **Resource 5.4 Data in**. They use **Sort** or **Filter** options to analyse the data. They use the **AND** option to interrogate the data further.

Module Task

Pupils load the data handling file they modified in Task 2. They list different questions that could be answered by the data in the file and that would be helpful in testing the hypothesis. They use **Sort** and **Filter** enquiries to extract data. They ask a partner to find the answers to the same questions and then compare results.

Task 4 (Red)

Pupils working at the higher level are asked to carry out more complex filtering of the data in **Resource 5.4 Data in** and to compare their results with a partner as a check.

Homework suggestion

Identify where errors were made in collecting or entering data and create a list of possible solutions.

Suggested extension activity

As an additional activity pupils could:

1 Load the latest version of their data handling file.

2 Identify areas where they think the layout could be improved; perhaps they need to make the titles larger, move blocks of data, change the colours.

3 Create a new worksheet and by copying and pasting the contents of the original file create their new layout.

4 Print the worksheet and annotate it to show why they have changed it.

Level guide

Level 5

Pupils working at Level 5 and above will be able to enter data into the data file efficiently, using software tools wherever possible. They will be able to work out methods to test the accuracy of data in the file including the use of column charts. They will interrogate a data file and be able to answer questions. They will be able to use sort routines and filtering data including the use of the **AND** operator. They will be able to create questions based upon their data with confidence and know how to direct others to use the file.

Level 4

Pupils working at Level 4 will enter their data into the data file. They will be able to interrogate a prepared file and make use of suitable software tools. They will know how to set up column charts to test the accuracy of the data. They will be able to use filtering when shown how to set up the conditions. They will be able to create questions that are dependent upon their own data files and to work with others to obtain the same answers.

Level 3

Pupils working at Level 3 and below will enter data into a prepared data file. They will be able to set up a column chart on the data and will be able to see whether there are any major mistakes and check accuracy. They will be able to find the answer to questions with help and understand how to sort data. They will be able to create a limited set of questions about their own data file.

Unit 5.6
Drawing conclusions from data

In this unit pupils learn how to draw conclusions from their database. They will select specific data for a report that contains evidence to support their conclusion.

Supports DfES sample teaching unit 7.5.6

ICT Framework Objectives

FINDING THINGS OUT

Organising and investigating

● *In an investigation:*
  – *investigate relationships between variables*
  – *check whether conclusions are plausible*
  – *review and amend the structure and its data to answer further questions.*

Suggested lesson plan

Starter
The Starter activities centre on the plausibility of data. They give the opportunity for pupils to consider whether statements can be tested and supported by data that can be collected.

Main part
Pupils consider methods they find the most plausible and easy to follow when drawing conclusions from a data file. They express their opinions about the different methods. The Module Task gives them the opportunity to draw up a list of conclusions about a hypothesis and to search and sort their data file to extract relevant data to support the conclusions that they make. They have to create graphs and charts to check for accuracy and to test the plausibility of what they are saying. Then they create a report in a word processing program. In Task 2, pupils working at the higher levels are asked to use a dynamic data link between their data file and the report so that if they change a value in the data file, the report will be automatically updated.

Key vocabulary
enquiry, record, search method, variable, viewpoint

Resources
Pupil Book: Module 5 Unit 5.6, pages 132–134
Resource 5.6 Music
Large computer screen display
Software for data handling, word processing and presentation

Plenary
Draw together the experiences of the class and discuss the stages involved from suggesting a hypothesis and planning the collection of data, to writing the report. Ask them to do Task 3 and write up the stages of developing the report.

Differentiation
Most pupils will be able to discuss the different methods of presenting data and describe the one that they prefer. They will be able to produce a report that states a basic conclusion. Differentiation occurs at the point where pupils draw realistic conclusions and find data to support them. Furthermore, more able pupils will attempt to describe the stages of producing the report from the first stages – working out a hypothesis, methods for checking the plausibility of data, and producing a report with text and graphics.

Suggested starters

1   Whole class discussion. The objective is to try to make pupils consider the plausibility of the statements and work out whether they could be tested and supported by data or not. Pupils are

asked whether they think these statements are plausible:

- Most people in hot countries wear shorts
- Britain has the largest population of house sparrows in the northern hemisphere
- Everest is one third as high again as any other mountain

2 Whole class activity. The objective of this activity is to make pupils think about a description of something and look more deeply at the meaning to see if it could be true.
Tell the class several riddles that sound untrue. They have to tell you which ones they believe are an accurate description of something and which have been made up. For example:

It has holes on the top and bottom, on the left and right, and in the middle, but it still holds water.   (A sponge)

It is as light as a feather, yet the strongest man can't hold it for much more than a minute. What is it?   (Breath)

3 Whole class activity. Before the activity place a small animal toy in your classroom but hidden from the pupils. Ask the pupils to close their eyes. While they have their eyes closed, make a few noises of opening cupboards and bags. Tell them to open their eyes and tell them that while they had their eyes shut you managed to persuade an 'X' (elephant/bear/crocodile, whatever the toy is) to hide in the front cupboard. Ask them if it is plausible, and only after you have had a series of different responses, reveal the truth of the matter.

Notes on Tasks

Task 1 (Green)
This task could be done as a whole class discussion. Display **Resource 5.6 Music** on the projector. Pupils decide as to whether the data and the questions there are reflected in the statements that accompany the data. They form judgements about which set of

statements is easier to understand and appears the most accurate. Draw out issues about how the data is displayed, as well as how to clear the various statements area.

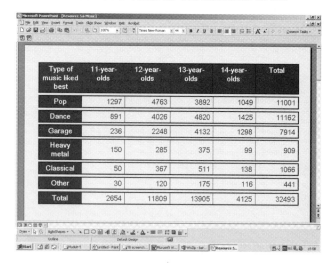

Would it be easier to understand the data if it was displayed graphically?

Module Task
Pupils create a report showing their conclusions about the hypothesis '12-year-olds have more foreign holidays today than they would have done in the 1970s'. They are asked to draw four conclusions from the data, and to provide evidence in the form of charts and tables to support these conclusions. The report is to be produced in a word processing package, so the data needs to be copied and pasted into the report. You should remind pupils that the survey they did was on a small local scale and that it might not reflect the national picture.

Task 2 (Red)
Pupils working at the higher level are asked to make use of a **Paste Special** link that will enable data to automatically change in the report if it is updated in the data file.

Task 3 (Green)
Pupils work with a partner to write a report on all the stages that have been necessary to create the final report which tests the hypothesis.

Homework suggestion

Write up the work from Task 3.

Suggested extension activity

As an additional activity pupils could:

1   Load the latest version of their data handling file.

2   Use the file to test out the hypothesis that '10% of 12-year-olds go away four times per year'.

3   Add data to their report that supports their conclusions about the new hypothesis.

4   Print out their amended report.

Level guide

Level 5

Pupils working at Level 5 and above will be able to make reasoned arguments as to which method of presenting data is the most accurate and easily accessible for most people. They will be able to question the plausibility of data that appears incorrect in statements. They will be able to interrogate the data file with confidence and produce a report that shows accuracy and relevant data to support their conclusions. They will be able to describe the stages of producing the report from the first stages of working out a hypothesis and mention methods they used for checking the plausibility of data as they worked.

Level 4

Pupils working at Level 4 will make judgements about how easy it is to understand data and statements taken from raw data. They will question the accuracy of statements. They will be able to create a report based upon data from their data file and copy and paste it between documents. They will draw realistic conclusions and find data to support them. They will be able to recall the stages of producing the report from the first development of a hypothesis, although the emphasis on accuracy may not be mentioned.

Level 3

Pupils working at Level 3 and below will be able to discuss the different methods of presenting data and describe the one that they prefer without justification. They will be able to produce a report, with help, that states a basic conclusion. They will make a list of the stages for producing the report when prompted.

Module 5
Are girls richer?

To complete Module 5 pupils are required to test out the following hypothesis:
'12-year-old girls get more pocket money than 12-year-old boys'

Resources

Pupil Book: Module 5, pages 111–137

Module 5 Assignment Evaluation form

Spreadsheet and word processing software

National Curriculum Level indicators based upon pupil outcome

Level indicators At the end of this assignment		
Pupils working at Level 3 will: • With help use the data supplied to create questions that will provide relevant responses • Create a basic questionnaire that will allow them to record responses • Need to be told who to get responses from • Enter data into a data file which has been created for them • Produce a graph from the data	Pupils working at Level 4 will: • Use a series of types of questions that are relevant to the given hypothesis • Create a questionnaire that will allow users to record their responses effectively • Create a data file using spreadsheet software that will allow the data to be searched and sorted to achieve desired results • Enter data into their data file and check its accuracy • Produce a graph and draw a conclusion about the hypothesis • Create a report which includes their graph and states their conclusion clearly	Pupils working at Level 5 will: • Use data supplied to work out a range of types of questions that would generate responses that would be useful to test the given hypothesis • Create a questionnaire that will allow data to be used effectively to test the hypothesis • Check and refine the questions to ensure that they are clear, unambiguous and allow for all possible responses • Select own sample showing an awareness of sample size and representation issues • Create a data file to record the responses from the questionnaire • Use the data to investigate the hypothesis. Identify patterns in the data and suggest valid interpretations for them • Use appropriate graphs and charts to illustrate their conclusions • Produce a well argued report of their conclusions using text and graphs • Check the validity of their conclusions using other sources • Suggest ways to improve the investigation to make the conclusions even more valid e.g. use a bigger sample or have additional questions to qualify the response

Module 6
Control and monitoring

Where this module fits in	Prior learning
This module builds on: Work done in KS2, particularly the 'Developing ideas, and making things happen' section.	Whilst it is not essential for this module it is likely that pupils starting this module will have experienced some aspects of control which may have included: ● programming a floor turtle ● testing and modifying a series of instructions to solve a problem ● writing simple procedures ● linking output devices together.
The main concept of this module is: To help pupils to understand that technology is used to control many everyday events. Pupils use software to simulate a range of familiar scenarios and to develop and refine flowcharts for control programs. The efficiency of the programs is enhanced through loops and subroutines.	
This module leads on to: Work on control technology in Student Books 2 and 3.	Revision of these areas is in Module 6 Prior learning section.

Subject knowledge needed by teachers	
To teach this module you will need to know how to:	Information on this aspect can be found in:
Load and save work in a shared area	Pupil Book pages 1, 24
Use a control box and sensors to model simple control scenarios	Pupil Book pages 138–139, 142, 148, 157–158 Resource 6.5 Control commands
Use programming software to control simple events, using decisions, loops and procedures	Pupil Book pages 144–145, 147, 151, 153–154, 158, 163 Resource 6.2 Buggy, Resource 6.4 Driving a car, Resource 6.5 Light flash
Knowledge of analogue and digital sensors	Pupil Book pages 107–108, 139, 142, 164–165 Resource 6.5 Pelican crossing

Level indicators
At the end of this module

Pupils working at Level 3 will:	Pupils working at Level 4 will:	Pupils working at Level 5 will:
• Work out a simple sequence of events to control a device • Choose a sensor without considering alternatives or evaluating the suitability of their choice • Create a simple linear sequence of control instruments to achieve a specific outcome	• Carefully plan a sequence of instructions to control events in a predetermined manner • Consider a range of sensors and make choices that they can justify • Build a control system, check it and make corrections so that it works as intended	• Monitor and measure external events with sensors • Try a range of ideas at the planning stage and develop and refine a plan based on reasoned choices • Employ a range of sensors to take account of different eventualities to make their system more effective • Build a control system carefully checking, correcting and refining it as they work • Use procedures or sub-tasks to construct, test and refine their system

Overview of module content and how it fits with the DfES sample teaching units			
Module in Pupil Book	Matches DfES lesson (in terms of content and and teaching objectives covered)	Outline of content	Progress on Module Task
Module 6 Prior learning PB pages 138–139		These pages prompt and help pupils to identify control activities they participated in at primary school.	
6.1 Control systems in everyday life PB pages 140–143 TB pages 119–122	Lesson 7.6.1	Understanding control in everyday life; study of car park barrier systems. Using instructions to control events. Automated systems: advantages/disadvantages. Input and output devices.	Developing a set of instructions. Advantages/disadvantages of control systems. Recognition of input and output devices
6.2 Using flowchart symbols and writing instructions PB pages 144–146 TB pages 123–127	Lesson 7.6.2	Uses of control systems. Flowcharts. Introduction to control software.	Development of sequential instructions. Introduction to use of flowcharts. Introduction to preferred control program (school's choice). Matching of flowchart symbols to preferred control program.
6.3 Using a sensor as a switch in a control model PB pages 147–149 TB pages 128–130	Lesson 7.6.3	Introduction to loops. If … then conditions. Use of input devices to increase safety. How a loop can improve the efficiency of a system.	Use of loops. Use of input devices. Using input devices to improve safety
6.4 Creating and testing control systems PB pages 150–152 TB pages 131–134	Lesson 7.6.4	Parallel processing. Develop multiprocessing programs using several variables.	Parallel processing. More complex systems
6.5 Creating an efficient system to monitor an event PB pages 153–155 TB pages 135–138	Lesson 7.6.5	Merging procedures, subroutines and subtasks.	Subroutines and procedures. Develop a system that others could use to control a buggy by using a toolbox of procedures.
Module 6 Assignment PB page 156 TB page 139	All of 7.6	Assignment covering the same learning objectives as those covered in Module 6 lessons, but in the context of designing a burglar proof jewel case to contain a precious stone. Scope for pupils to perform at Levels 3, 4 and 5.	

Cross curricular opportunities	
Subject	Programme of study section
Science 2 (life processes) Design and Technology PE	3a (logging data using sensors in experiments on photosynthesis) 5a–g (knowledge about control systems) 4a–d (monitoring heart, pulse, etc) 7a–c (use video/data logging to record performance levels)

Unit 6.1
Control systems in everyday life

In this unit pupils make a control system by writing sets of instructions to control a car park barrier. They learn about procedures and repeated processes.

Supports DfES sample teaching unit 7.6.1

ICT Framework objectives

DEVELOPING IDEAS AND MAKING THINGS HAPPEN

Control and monitoring

- Implement a system to carry out a simple control task by:
  – compiling sets of instructions
  – identifying those instructions that can be grouped to form procedures or loops.

Key vocabulary

automatic, control, precise, procedure, program, programmer, repeated process, sequence of instructions

Suggested lesson plan

Starter

In the Starters pupils discuss what is meant by an automated system and consider the control systems involved. They discuss how automated systems might work and describe the step-by-step procedures involved.

Main part

Task 2 involves pupils listing advantages and disadvantages of using automated systems. In Task 1 pupils recognise the need to sequence activities in the right order and appreciate the need for precision which leads neatly to the Module Task. The main aim here is to reinforce the fact that any control system requires a precise sequence of events. Pupils are also introduced to the variety of input and output

Resources

Pupil Book: Module 6 Unit 6.1, pages 140–143
Resource 6 Flowchart outline
Resource 6.1 Automation
Resource 6.1 Control in the kitchen
Resource 6.1 Bikes
Resource 6.1 Input
Resource 6.1 Amazing machines
Resource 6.1 Barrier 1
Resource 6.1 Barrier 2
Movie-playing software, such as Windows Media Player or Quicktime

devices that could be used in a control system. Task 3 reinforces the Module Task, but also aims to exploit the skills already gained by allowing pupils to improve the system by adding additional safety and security features. Task 4 also aims to introduce the wide range of sensors that are available to control systems and encourages students to think of appropriate uses for each sensor.

Plenary

Bring the class together to revisit Task 2 and discuss the advantages and disadvantages of automated systems. Ask if they had thought of any more during the lesson. Suggest the homework activity to help pupils identify control systems and recognise advantages and disadvantages of control systems in their own home.

Differentiation

Most pupils will know about input and output devices and will be able to give an example of each. They will be able to produce a sequence of instructions in response to a given problem. More able pupils can go on to assess the validity of their work and make any required improvements. Ask them how they would make their programs more efficient.

Suggested starters

1 Whole class discussion, then pairs. Discuss with pupils what is meant by an automated system. Ask them about automated systems around the school: burglar alarms, automatic lights, CCTV, heating systems. Ask the pupils to work in pairs to create a list of automated systems in the home.

2 Whole class discussion. Ask pupils if they did any control work in their primary school. Ask them to refer to the Pupil Book and see if they recognise the Pixie or the Roamer on page 138. Ask them what they actually did.

3

Whole class discussion. Show pupils **Resource 6.1 Amazing machines** which displays some incredible machines and inventions. If necessary, access more via http://www.heinemann.co.uk/hotlinks. Discuss how they might work. Ask pupils to choose one and describe how it works in a step-by-step way.

Notes on Tasks

Task 1 (Green)

This activity is best done in pairs. Pupils are asked to watch **Resource 6.1 Bikes** which shows the stages which lead to riding a bike. They watch the video as many times as required and write a list of instructions starting with 'Push the bike from the garden to the side of the road,' up to the point when they are riding down the road.

The key desired outcome is that pupils recognise the need to sequence activities in the right order and appreciate the need for precision.

Task 2 (Green)

Pupils make a list of the advantages and disadvantages of using automated systems. Give them the worksheet **Resource 6.1 Automation** to record their work.

(Advantages may include: quality control, cheaper than employing a person, removes boring work from humans, safety, can work where humans can't (in hazardous areas) such as a bomb disposal robot.
Disadvantages may include: loss of jobs, loss of skills, no spontaneous thought, no imagination.)

Module Task

Task 3 (Red)

Pupils watch a second video of a slightly different car barrier system, **Resource 6.1 Barrier 2**. This activity reinforces the Module Task, but also aims to exploit the skills already gained by allowing pupils to improve on the system shown by adding additional safety and security features.

Task 4 (Green)

Pupils watch the video of a car barrier system, **Resource 6.1 Barrier 1**. They write down the sequence of events which makes the barrier work on the worksheet, **Resource 6 Flowchart outline**. Pupils then annotate their flowchart with the input and output devices in a car barrier system. The main aim of this task is to reinforce the idea that any control system needs a precise sequence of events programmed into the device, and to introduce pupils to input and output devices.

Pupils consider a wide range of sensors that are available to control systems and encouraged to think of appropriate uses of each sensor. Hand out the worksheet **Resource 6.1 Input** for them to record their notes.

Homework

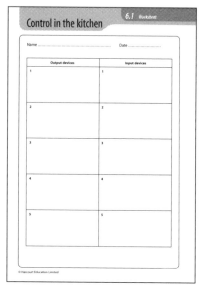

Ask the pupils to list three input and three output devices used in their kitchen at home. They should list them on the worksheet **Resource 6.1 Control in the kitchen**.

Input devices may include: light switches, push switch on the fridge door, heating thermostat, toaster with timer.
Output devices: motors driving a variety of appliances, elements in an oven, kettle element, extractor fan.

Suggested extension activity

Design a Heath Robinson-type contraption that makes use of modern input and output devices. It does not need to have any real practical use, it could just be an amusing toy.

Level guide

Level 5
Pupils working at Level 5 will be able to describe the difference between an input and output device and give examples of each. They will have an understanding of appropriate uses of a range of sensors. They will be able to sequence a set of instructions and assess the validity of their work and make any required improvements. They will recognise that procedures can be used to produce a more efficient program.

Level 4
Pupils working at Level 4 will know about input and output devices and will be able to give an example of each. They will be able to produce a sequence of instructions in response to a given problem. They will be able to provide an example of a suitable application of one or two sensors.

Level 3
Pupils working at Level 3 will be able to produce a sequence of instructions in response to a given problem. They will know the difference between an input and output device.

Unit 6.2

Using flowchart symbols and writing instructions

In this unit pupils learn how to use a flowchart for creating programs.

Supports DfES sample teaching unit 7.6.2

ICT Framework objectives

DEVELOPING IDEAS AND MAKING THINGS HAPPEN

Analysing and automating processes

● *Represent simple processes as diagrams showing:*
  – *how a task can be broken down into smaller ones.*
  – *the sequence of operations, and any conditions or decisions that affect it*
  – *the initial information needed.*

Key vocabulary

decision, efficient, flowchart, input, logic, output, process, program, sequence of instructions, start, stop

Suggested lesson plan

Starters

The Starters centre on control instructions and the order in which they should be given for a number of humorous machines or a recipe. This is followed by a class discussion where a task can be used to illustrate quite detailed instructions even though it might be a simple task.

Main part

The aim of Task 1 is to identify the types of systems best undertaken by an automated system. These include repetitive operations, dangerous situations and safety systems. Those systems best undertaken by humans are those that are continually changing where there is a need for interaction with other humans, or when creativity and imagination are involved.

Resources

Pupil Book: Module 6 Unit 6.2, pages 144–146
Resource 6 Flowchart outline
Resource 6.2 Buggy
Resource 6.2 Litter machine
Resource 6.2 Litter picking
Resource 6.2 Sausage stroganoff
Resource 6.2 Recipe
Resource 6.2 How do you …
Resource 6.2 Inventions
Resource 6.2 Flowchart for window cleaner – for teacher only
Resource 6.2 Flowchart for picture snapping machine – for teacher only
Resource 6.2 Instructions
Resource 6.2 Gum flowchart
Resource 6.2 Flowchart planning sheet
Software for word processing and presentations
A control and monitoring package that allows onscreen simulations, for example, Flowol, Logicator or Crocodile Clips, Robolab, or any suitable control software

Task 2 is geared to reinforce previous work to encourage pupils to reduce their commands to the minimum and to introduce the concepts of a loop and decision box. The Module Task follows and encourages the pupils to break down the task into small single action steps. They then use the correct flowchart symbols to structure their solution to simulate the normal programming procedure. In Task 3 the more able pupils are presented with the challenge of writing a program to drive a buggy. If school facilities allow, pupils could test their program using the school control and monitoring software.

Plenary

Bring together the work in the unit by having a class discussion on the control instructions used for programs to drive machines (or buggies). Reinforce the use of each flowchart symbol. Ask the pupils to consider how they would change their programs to achieve the minimum number of commands. This will introduce the concept of repeat instructions and subroutines which are covered in the next unit.

Differentiation

Most pupils will know the main flowchart symbols and will be able to break a task down into a number of steps and construct a simple flowchart solution to a given task. Some pupils may need help in constructing their flowcharts where more able pupils can be asked to exploit decision boxes and repeated processes. More able pupils will be able to evaluate what they have done and make improvements based on these evaluations.

Suggested starters

1

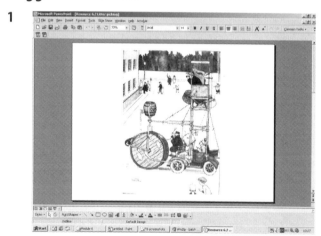

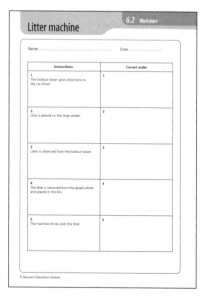

Whole class discussion. Show the Heath Robinson machine from **Resource 6.2 Litter picking**. Discuss what the machine is actually doing. Show the list of activities on the second slide and ask pupils to list the activities in the best order using the worksheet **Resource 6.2 Litter machine**. Ask the pupils how the machine could be improved. Perhaps some control over the glue?

2

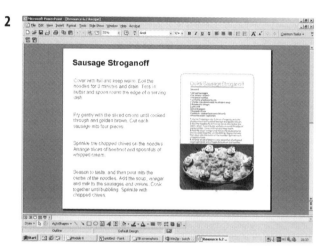

Whole class discussion. Use the recipe for sausage stroganoff from **Resource 6.2 Recipe** and ask pupils to place the instructions in the right order using the worksheet **Resource 6.2 Sausage stroganoff**. The four sections need reordering as well as the sentences within each section. You should ask pupils if there should be any time gaps between each activity.

3

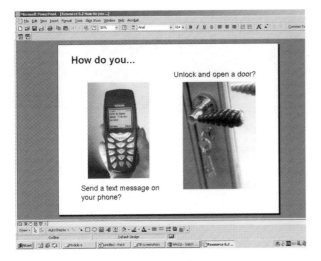

Pupils work in pairs followed by a class discussion. Ask the pairs of pupils to select one task from **Resource 6.2 How do you …** and write a series of instructions to do that task using the worksheet, **Resource 6.2 Instructions**. Give them 5–10 minutes to do this and then have a class discussion. It should be explained that the simplest task can require quite detailed instructions.

Notes on Tasks

Task 1 (Green)

This activity is best done in pairs or small groups. Pupils list activities that are best done by automatic control systems and those best done by humans.

The aim is to identify the types of systems best undertaken by an automated system. These include repetitive operations, dangerous situations and safety systems.

Those systems best undertaken by humans are those that are continually changing or where there is a need for interaction with other

humans. Humans are also better than automated systems when creativity and imagination are involved.

Task 2 (Green)

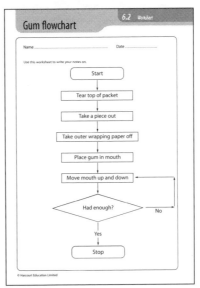

Pupils work on the worksheet **Resource 6.2 Gum flowchart** to amend and improve a flowchart that describes chewing gum. Then give out the worksheet **Resource 6 Flowchart outline** for pupils to write out their revised flowchart in full.

This task should encourage pupils to reduce the number of commands to a minimum and introduces the concepts of a loop and decision box.

Module Task

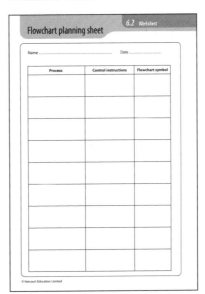

This activity is best done in pairs or small groups. Pupils use the worksheet, **Resource 6.2 Flowchart planning sheet** to plan instructions for making toast. They then use the correct flowchart symbols to structure their solution to simulate the normal programming procedure. They should be encouraged to consider the use of subroutines.

This task encourages pupils to break down the event into small single-action steps.

Task 3 (Red)

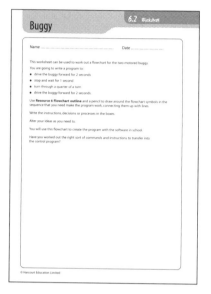

Pupils plan a control program to drive a buggy. Give them the worksheets **Resource 6.2 Buggy** and **Resource 6 Flowchart outline** to assist pupils in creating a simple flowchart. They will need to realise that the only way they can control the buggy is by turning the motors on and off for different amounts of time.

They should consider the best way of turning the buggy. (This can be done in two ways: just turning on one motor or by turning both motors on but rotating in different directions.)

Many pupils forget to put a time delay in between turning the motor on and off. You should explain to pupils that a computer executes each instruction in a tiny fraction of a second.

If pupils have access to a computer interface box and a buggy they should test their solution.

Homework

Give out the worksheet **Resource 6.2 Inventions** which shows two drawings of humorous machines by Rube Goldberg. Ask pupils to select one and produce a flowchart that shows the sequence of events that each machine undertakes. Give them the worksheet, **Resource 6 Flowchart outline** to record their solution. (Compare with worksheets **Resource 6.2 Picture snapping solution** and **Resource 6.2 Window cleaning solution**, which are also shown here.)

You could help pupils by discussing the 'window cleaning' machine. Ask them which of the commands listed below the pictures are inputs and which are user interaction.

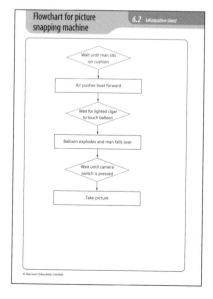

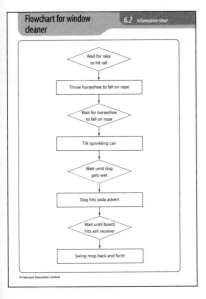

Flowchart for window cleaner — 6.2 *Information sheet*

Suggested extension activity

Pupils could design their own incredible machine, listing inputs, output and user interaction. Some possible ideas could be a machine to:

- brush the classroom floor
- take books to a teacher's car
- mark examination papers
- replace the goalkeeper in their favourite football team.

Level guide

Level 5

Pupils working at Level 5 will understand and make good use of flowchart symbols. They will appreciate and be able to exploit decision boxes and repeated processes. They will be able to break down a task into a sequence of small single action steps. They will be able to evaluate what they have done and make improvements based on these evaluations.

Level 4

Pupils working at Level 4 will know the main flowchart symbols and will be able to implement a simple flowchart solution to a given task. They should be able to break a task down into a number of steps.

Level 3

Pupils working at Level 3 understand a completed flowchart simulation but will need help in constructing their own system.

Unit 6.3
Using a sensor as a switch in a control model

In this unit pupils learn how to create a set of instructions to control an output device in response to physical data that has been recorded by a sensor.

Supports DfES sample teaching unit 7.6.3

ICT Framework objectives

DEVELOPING IDEAS AND MAKING THINGS HAPPEN

Control and monitoring

● *Implement a system to carry out a simple control task, including some that involve sensed physical data, by:*
  – *compiling sets of instructions, identifying those which can be grouped to form procedures or loops*
  – *testing and refining the instructions.*

Key vocabulary

automate, if … then, input, input device, loop, output, output device, procedure, system

Suggested lesson plan

Starter
The Starter activities are all examples of situations that use a control interface. Choose the one(s) that best suits the equipment in the school. In each case pupils should recognise that sensors are used to control events.

Main part
Task 1 introduces pupils to the use of loops as they study a pelican crossing system. These are also used in Task 2, which utilises loops and decision boxes in writing a flowchart to represent the movement of a lift. The purpose of the Module Task is to let pupils develop knowledge of the range and type of sensors that are available and how sensors are used to control output devices to increase safety. Task 4 allows pupils to consolidate what they have learnt by applying their knowledge to a new situation. They are asked to identify a dangerous area or utensil in the kitchen and design a system to improve the safety of that device.

Resources
Pupil Book: Module 6 Unit 6.3, pages 147–149
Resources 6 Flowchart outline
Resource 6.3 Crossing
Resource 6.3 Car safety
Computer and large display
Software for word processing and presentations
A control and monitoring package that allows onscreen simulations, for example, Flowol, Logicator Robolab or Crocodile Clips, or any suitable control software
A webcam with movement-sensor software
A control box (depending on your choice of software)

Task 3 offers the opportunity for the more able pupils to extend the Module Task by writing instructions that control output devices when the safety feature is activated. For example if the car door is open a warning light comes on.

Plenary
Review the lesson by reminding pupils that sensors can control output devices and that the flowcharts they have created could be used with an interface to control an automated system.

Differentiation
Task 2 is an example of a task that utilises loops and decision boxes, in what can be a difficult or easy problem. The difficulty of this task is dependent on the number of floors the lift has to visit. You can differentiate this task by asking most pupils to devise a system for a lift with a ground and first floor. More able pupils can then extend the system by one or more floors.

Suggested starters

1   Whole class discussion. Use a sound sensor connected to an interface box to measure the sound in the classroom. When there is little sound one bulb is lit, but as the sound increases more bulbs are turned on.
(This could be easily demonstrated with the Logicator software and the smart box interface.)

2   Whole class discussion. Use a temperature sensor controlling a cooling fan in the classroom.
(There is a standard model provided with the LEGO control lab, but it can be easily used with Robolab.)

3   Whole class discussion. Build a buggy with touch/push sensors on the front and back of the model. Program the buggy to go back and forth between two walls.
(If you have the Robolab software there is a bumper car model in the 'Amusement Park' set.)

In each case pupils should recognise that sensors are used to control events.

Notes on Tasks

Task 1 (Green)

This task introduces the use of loops. Pupils watch **Resource 6.3 Crossing** and then create a flowchart to simulate the pelican crossing. They can use the worksheet **Resource 6 Flowchart Outline** to help them create the flowchart. Remind them that it will need to have at least one loop.

Task 2 (Green)

Pupils work with a partner to write a sequence of instructions for a lift that goes up and down. This task utilises loops and decision boxes, in what can be a difficult or easy problem. The difficulty of this task is dependent on the number of floors the lift has to visit. You can differentiate this task by asking pupils to devise a system for a lift with one floor and then extend the system by one or more floors. All pupils should produce a flowchart for a lift with just a ground and first floor in the first instance, using the worksheet **Resource 6 Flowchart outline** to help them.

Module Task

Pupils consider the safety sensors used on a car, annotating the worksheet **Resource 6.3 Car safety** as they work. Then they choose an additional safety feature, decide on the type of sensors they need and design the flowchart to control it (utilising the worksheet **Resource 6 Flowchart outline**). The purpose of this task is to allow pupils to develop knowledge of the range and type of sensors that are available and how sensors are used to control output devices to increase safety.

Task 3 (Red)

In this task pupils extend the Module Task to control output devices when the safety feature is activated. For example, if the car door is open the car will make a sound and/or turn on a warning light, and the engine will not start.

Pupils should be encouraged to think of the pros and cons of excessive control systems. For example, is it wise to make the car inoperable just because a door push sensor has failed?

Task 4 (Green)

Pupils consolidate what they have learnt by applying their knowledge to a new situation. They identify a dangerous area or utensil in the kitchen and design a system to improve the safety of that device.

Pupils might search the Internet to find which accidents occur most often and design a system that addresses the most common accident. A useful starting point may be accessed via http://www.heinemann.co.uk/hotlinks.

They should produce a suitable flowchart using the worksheet **Resource 6 Flowchart outline** and identify which types of sensors they would use.

Homework suggestion

Pupils could complete Task 4.

Suggested extension activity

Pupils could try to design and make their own sensor for a particular job. The sensors could be used:

- to test the weight of a letter to make sure it's not too heavy for a first class stamp

- to switch on a light when a cat comes through the cat flap.

The sensors could be made with two paper plates, each covered in cooking foil with a wire protruding from the middle. Foam rings of differing thickness can fit over the wires, preventing them from touching the facing plate when they are placed together. The foam acts as a pressure mat. Applying gentle pressure to the bottom of each plate will compress the foam rings, allowing the wires to reach the opposite plate, touch the foil and complete the circuit. The thickness of the foam can be varied to make the sensor more or less sensitive. Obviously these sensors cannot be linked to a light or a buzzer, but they may help pupils to visualise the sensors they are trying to write control systems for. Pupils could use **Resource 6 Flowchart outline** and write a system to match their newly designed sensor.

Level guide

Level 5

Pupils working at Level 5 will be aware of a range of sensors and their appropriate uses. They will be aware that sensors can control output devices. They will be able to recognise the advantages and disadvantages of an automated control system and be able to suggest ways that control systems could be used in the world around them. They will be able to discuss and implement solutions to quite complex systems, for example, a lift with three or four floors.

Level 4

Pupils working at Level 4 will be aware of a range of sensors and their appropriate uses. They will be aware that sensors can control output devices. They will be able to devise a system that operates a lift with two floors.

Level 3

Pupils working at Level 3 will be aware of a range of sensors and their appropriate uses. They will be able to devise a simple flowchart where a sensor controls one output device.

Unit 6.4

Creating and testing control systems

In this unit pupils learn how to create and test control systems on a computer.

Supports DfES sample teaching unit 7.6.4

ICT Framework objectives

DEVELOPING IDEAS AND MAKING THINGS HAPPEN

Analysing and automating processes

● *Represent simple processes as diagrams, showing:*
   – *how a task can be broken down into smaller ones*
   – *the sequence of operations, and any conditions or decisions that affect it*
   – *the initial information needed.*

Control and monitoring

● *Implement a system to carry out a simple control task, including some that involve sensed physical data, by:*
   – *compiling sets of instructions, identifying those which can be grouped to form procedures or loops*
   – *testing and refining the instructions.*

Key vocabulary

improve, procedure, refine, subtask, switch, system

Resources

Pupil Book: Module 6 Unit 6.4, pages 150–154

Resource 6.4 Automated room

Resource 6.4 Driving a car

Resource 6.4 Simple procedure

Resource 6.4 Automated greenhouse

Resource 6.4 Castle map

Resource 6.4 Castle security

Resource 6 Flowchart outline

Software for word processing and presentations

A control and monitoring package that allows onscreen simulations, for example, Flowol, Logicator or Crocodile Clips, Robolab, or any suitable control software

A control box (depending on your choice of software)

Suggested lesson plan

Starter

The Starter suggestions prompt pupils to consider several everyday scenarios and the number of parallel activities that each one involves. They are introduced to the concept of multitasking and parallel processing.

Main part

The purpose of Task 1 is to relate real control activities to a flowchart system and to help pupils begin to realise the need for multitasking programming. The task also reinforces the use of loops and conditional statements. This leads neatly into the Module Task which is designed to help pupils to develop a control system. They devise a flowchart for each requirement, which are written as subroutines or procedures. Then Task 2 allows them to develop a master program executing each subroutine or procedure once a single input device has been

activated. This establishes the concept of a master program calling up a number of subroutines. In Task 3 and/or 4 pupils develop a system that requires an understanding of the requirements of the sensors needed for continuous monitoring of these conditions.

Plenary

Review all pupils' work on multitasking and parallel processing, understanding master programs that execute a number of subroutines, and the sensors required for continuous monitoring of selected situations. Ask them to consider possible ways that we could use ICT systems to help check our health. This activity could allow the pupils working towards the higher levels to come up with innovative ideas.

Differentiation

Most pupils will have an understanding that output devices can be controlled and activated by input sensors and will be able to create the subroutines required to control a system containing these. The challenge will be presented when they come to check and refine their systems. Many may need assistance and will benefit from examples and demonstrations, but the more able will be able to analyse their systems and demonstrate their solutions using a control interface and some sensors, and then relate these to a commercial task.

Suggested starters

1   Whole class discussion. Ask all the class to tap their heads whilst rubbing their stomach in a circular movement. Doing two different things at the same time can be very difficult. Doing three is even harder! Ask them to tap their foot at the same time: if they can do this it's called parallel processing or multitasking. They are trying to get their brain to run three programs at the same time as well as pumping their heart, breathing and so on. The human body is a true multitasking machine.

Ask pupils to think of any other situations where a number of programs need to run at the same time.

2

Ask pupils to look at the flowchart on the worksheet, **Resource 6.4 Simple procedure**. What is the program for? (It is a very simplified set of procedures to drive a car.) Then show them the slide show in **Resource 6.2 Driving a car**. Ask pupils to describe the subroutine for changing gear when stopping? (A solution is hyperlinked within the Resource.)

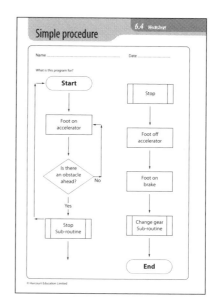

Ask the pupils what other processes the driver should be thinking about whilst driving. A number of possibilities are suggested on slide 3. Explain that when we have several tasks running at the same time it is called multitasking or parallel processing.

Notes on Tasks

Task 1 (Green)

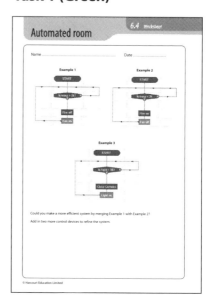

Pupils look at three control systems in an automated room. Give out the worksheet **Resource 6.4 Automated room** and ask pupils to improve and refine the system. A possible solution is shown overleaf.

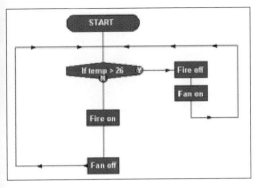

Module Task

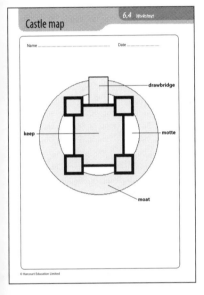

Pupils design an alarm system for the Queen's castle. Give them a plan of the castle from **Resource 6.4 Castle map** and ask them to complete questions a–c from the Pupil Book using this worksheet.

This task is designed to help pupils to develop a control system. Pupils should devise a flowchart for each sensor by using the worksheet **Resource 6 Flowchart outline**.

There are some flowcharts on the second slide of **Resource 6.4 Castle security** to prompt pupils.

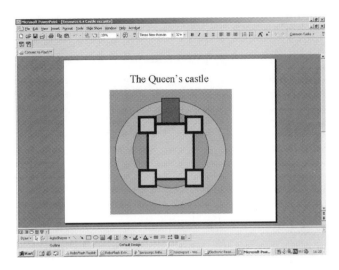

Task 2 (Red)

More able pupils use their knowledge of flowcharts, loops and parallel processing to operate the security system designed in the Module Task at the touch of a button. This establishes the concept of a master program calling up a number of subroutines. An example is given below.

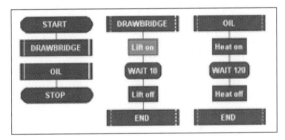

Task 3 (Green)

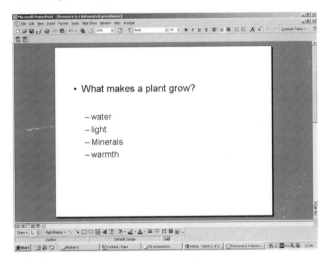

Pupils look at **Resource 6.4 Automated greenhouse**. They develop a greenhouse system that would allow flowers to be grown the whole year round. They first consider what is required for healthy flowers to be grown. Once they understand the requirements they can consider the sensors required to monitor these conditions. They create flowcharts to control each condition. Use the worksheet, **Resource 6 Flowchart outline** if required. If an interface and sensors are available, pupils could demonstrate one or two of their solutions.

As in Task 2 they should finish by bringing together all the routines under one central program. Some less able pupils will struggle to finish this task. You could try grouping them with more able pupils for support, or run a modified version of the task for these pupils with more support from you.

Task 4 (Green)

Pupils first consider the best ways to check how healthy people are. Suggestions could include a timed sprint or a set number of star jumps in a minute. The conditions used to measure health could include weight/height ratio, blood pressure, lung capacity, heart rate before and after exercise. Once the requirements are established, pupils should consider the sensors required to monitor the conditions. For example, to measure heart rate, they could use a sensor on the pulse and a timing device on a loop to measure heart beats until a set time is up. They create a flowchart and write a program to monitor one of the conditions. This task could be used as a project for assessment purposes, with pupils carrying out additional research into youth fitness levels, or factors which may affect the results of their tests, such as diet and lifestyle.

Homework

Pupils could complete Task 4.

Suggested extension activity

Pupils could design an automated lawnmower. They should consider the multi-tasking activities required for a mower to work effectively and safely.

They should write down a list of subroutines required in order that the whole lawn can be cut successfully.

Some questions to consider:

- Is the grass box full?
- Is there a person in front of me?
- Is there an obstacle in front of me?
- Is that a flower?

Level guide

Level 5

Pupils working at Level 5 will be able to understand the potential of an automated system. They will be aware of sensors that can be used to control a wide range of environmental conditions. They will be able to break the system down into manageable subroutines. They will be able to demonstrate some of their solutions using a control interface and some sensors and relate this to a commercial task.

Level 4

Pupils working at Level 4 will be able to create the subroutines required to control a specified system. They should be able to check and refine their own and others' work. They will be able to select which sensor is most appropriate to the task.

Level 3

Pupils working at Level 3 will produce flowcharts with help and have an understanding that output devices can be controlled and activated by input sensors.

Unit 6.5

Creating an efficient system to monitor an event

In this unit pupils will learn how to make a control program more efficient by breaking down a problem into procedures or subroutines.

Supports DfES sample teaching unit 7.6.5

ICT Framework objectives

DEVELOPING IDEAS AND MAKING THINGS HAPPEN

Analysing and automating processes
● *Represent simple processes as diagrams, showing:*
– *how a task can be broken down into smaller ones*
– *the sequence of operations, and any conditions or decisions that affect it*
– *the initial information needed.*

Control and monitoring
● *Implement a system to carry out a simple control task, including some that involve sensed physical data, by:*
– *compiling sets of instructions, identifying those which can be grouped to form procedures or loops*
– *testing and refining the instructions.*

Key vocabulary
improve, procedure, refine, subroutine, subtask, switch, system

Resources
Pupil Book: Module 6 Unit 6.5, pages 153–155
Resource 6.3 Crossing (from earlier Unit)
Resource 6.5 Pelican crossing
Resource 6.5 Light flash
Resource 6.5 Control commands
Software for word processing and presentations
A control and monitoring package that allows onscreen simulations, for example, Flowol, Logicator, Robolab or Crocodile Clips, or any suitable control software
A control box (depending on your choice of software)
LEGO buggy

Suggested lesson plan

Starter
Starter 1 gives pupils the opportunity to investigate the programming involved in a system with a flashing light. The concept of a time delay is introduced. Omission of this is a typical error pupils make when programming procedures, so it needs careful consideration.

Main part
Pupils are reminded that procedure, subtask and subroutine all have the same meaning. Task 1 identifies the benefits of subroutines. The Module Task offers the opportunity for pupils to put their knowledge into practice by asking the pupils to write a set of core subroutines to control a buggy and then use them in a number of different master programs. Task 3 brings together all the elements of control systems that the pupils have learnt in Module 6: inputs (taking in information), processes (making decisions from this information) and outputs (a result of the decision).

Plenary
Discuss with the class the sort of automated systems already in use in homes. Challenge them to think about adding some control systems into their bedroom to make their life easier. Suggest some inventions and contraptions similar to those in *Wallace and Grommit*. After 5–10 minutes receive feedback. Ask them to do homework based on these discussions and use a flowchart to demonstrate their solution.

Differentiation
Most pupils will be able to order subroutines to control a device and understand that the subroutines can make programming easier to write and test. More able pupils will be able to break a problem down into smaller parts and create subroutines to operate a system. The challenge to many will be to test, modify and improve the system and go on to design sophisticated systems that exploit a range of sensors to meet a specified need.

Suggested starters

1

Show pupils the first slide from **Resource 6.5 Light flash**. This procedure has been written to flash a light. Will it work? Explain that it will work but the flash will be so quick that they won't be able to see it, it will appear permanently on. So a delay is required. Show the second slide. Will this work? Explain that it will not really work either because there is no delay between turning the motor off and on. This is a typical error pupils make when programming so it needs careful consideration. Slide 3 gives a solution to the problem.

2 Ask pupils to write a set of instructions to program the body to move from their desk to the door. For this task, assume the body only knows the following words: stand, move, leg, left, right, turn right, turn left. But explain pupils can teach it new words that use the words it already knows. For example, **Walk** could be:

Walk
    Move left leg forward
    Move right leg forward
End walk

Give them five minutes to consider this problem. Ask pupils for their suggestions and find out what was the least number of commands needed.
Use this to introduce the concept of subroutines that can be used several times and so reduce the need for unnecessary coding.

Notes on Tasks

Task 1 (Green)

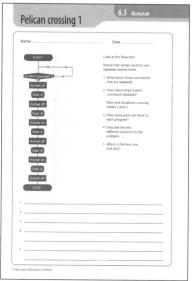

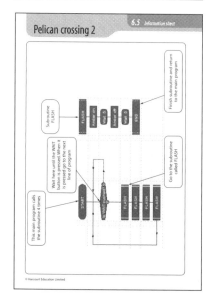

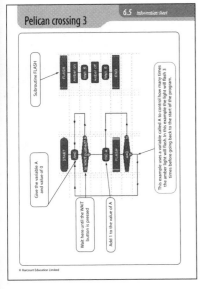

Pupils watch **Resource 6.3 Crossing**. They then look at the worksheet **Resource 6.5 Pelican crossing**. and note down the repeated sections in the first program on the worksheet. After looking at the second and third sheets within **Resource 6 Pelican crossing**, they can complete the questions on the worksheet.

Explain to the pupils that there are a number of words that mean subroutines. Procedure, subtask and subroutine all mean more or less the same. The purpose of this task is to identity the benefits of subroutines: that they avoid unnecessary duplication of program code and make it easier to read and test. Testing a small section at a time is much quicker and easier to debug. Subroutines can also be used in a variety of programming projects.

For example, Microsoft only ever writes one dictionary that can be used by all their programs.

Module Task

Working in pairs, pupils devise a set of core subroutines to control a variety of buggy movements. This task demonstrates the benefits of subroutines by asking pupils to use the subroutines in a number of different master programs.

This activity would be much enhanced if the pupils had access to buggies and control interfaces. The Helpsheet, **Resource 6.5 Control commands** will be useful for pupils who use LEGO RCX, Flowol and/or Logicator and, **Resource 6 Flowchart outline** is useful for those who require a flowchart worksheet.

If you are short of desktop space use a model that is static, for example a merry-go-round. Procedures could spin it left, spin right, go up, go down, vary the speed, do jerks and so on.

Task 2 (Red)

This is an extension of the Module Task for more able pupils. Pupils write two subroutines. The first turns the motors off when the buggy hits the wall, the second reverses the buggy and makes it turn when it hits a wall. Use the worksheet, **Resource 6 Flowchart outline**, if required.

These procedures could be used to program a buggy to find its way out of a maze.

This could become a competition activity: *Who can program their buggy to escape the maze the quickest?*

Task 3 (Green)

This task brings together all that pupils have learnt during the module. It can be done in small groups. Pupils must program a microwave oven with a series of instructions. This task gives more practice in writing subroutines. Encourage pupils to make their instructions as efficient as possible. Use the worksheet, **Resource 6 Flowchart outline** if required.

Homework

Pupils could work out systems for making their bedroom fully automated.

Suggested extension activity

Pupils could consider how to improve a pelican crossing system. They should try to solve the problem of cars waiting for the crossing lights to turn green when no one is actually crossing the road. You should explain that the control system of a pelican crossing is simplistic; that it uses a timing system rather than looking to see if anyone is actually waiting to cross the road. Pupils should devise additional sensors and systems to improve the pelican crossing so there are never any unnecessary delays.

Level guide

Level 5

Pupils working at Level 5 will be able to break a problem down into its constituent parts, which will have been used to produce a set of subroutines to control a device. In many cases they will be able to break down the problem into single event activities. They will be able to test, modify and improve the system. Using the skills they have gained, they will be able to design sophisticated systems that exploit a range of sensors to meet a specified need. They will recognise the advantages and disadvantages of automated control systems.

Level 4

Pupils working at Level 4 will be able to break a problem down into smaller parts, which will have been used to produce a set of subroutines to control a device. They will recognise the advantages and disadvantages of automated control systems.

Level 3

Pupils working at Level 3 will be able to order pre-created subroutines to control a device. They will understand that subroutines can make programming easier to write and test.

Module 6
Jewel show

Assignment

To complete Module 6 pupils are asked to design an alarm system to protect a valuable jewel that is on show to the public.

Resources

Pupil Book: Module 6, pages 138–163

Module 6 Assignment Evaluation form

Paper and drawing equipment for ideas and drawings of their system

Access to control simulation software and where possible control interface device and range of sensors for pupils to use to experiment

National Curriculum Level indicators based upon pupil outcome

Level indicators At the end of this assignment		
Pupils working at Level 3 will: • Work out a simple sequence of events that would trigger an alarm response to a sensor signal • Produce a simple diagram showing the intended sequence of events • Choose a sensor and alarm without considering alternatives or evaluating the suitability of their choice • Create a simple linear sequence of control instructions to activate an alarm	Pupils working at Level 4 will: • Carefully plan a sequence of instructions that would trigger an alarm in response to a sensor signal • Produce a flowchart that closely represents their plan • Consider a range of sensors and alarms and make choices that they can justify for the intended task • Build a control system, check it and make corrections so that it works as intended • Use a loop in their system so that the sensor(s) are checked continually	Pupils working at Level 5 will: • Try a range of ideas at the planning stage and develop a plan based upon reasoned choices • Produce a flowchart that accurately represents their plan and check it through carefully, identifying refinements and making corrections • Employ a range of sensors and/or alarms to take account of different eventualities to make their system more efficient and effective • Build a control system carefully, repeatedly checking it and making corrections • Use procedures or sub-tasks to construct and test separate component parts of the system • Identify and implement revisions and refinements to their system • Evaluate how well their finished system might work in real life, looking for flaws and weaknesses and identifying ways of improvement

Appendix
Data logging

Data logging is covered in Unit 7 of the QCA Scheme of Work, which is identified as a Year 7 unit. However, the Framework Yearly Teaching Objectives and the DfES sample teaching units both put it into the beginning of Year 8.

In *ICT Matters*, data logging will be covered in detail at the beginning of Year 8. However, we have included this short appendix which can be used as an introduction to the topic if teachers wish to introduce it in Year 7.

It is assumed that some teaching will have been done on the various types of sensors in Module 6. This appendix focuses mainly on setting up a data logging experiment and deciding the logging interval and logging period.

Task (green)

In the task, pupils look at **Resource Pondweed** – a set of real data collected during a simple science experiment. The purpose is to familiarise them with the type of data which is collected during data logging and to show how ICT can help interpret that data. They use skills learned in Modules 4 and 5 to present the data as a graph and draw some basic conclusions from it. More able students are asked to consider ways in which the data might be refined in order to make it easier to draw conclusions.

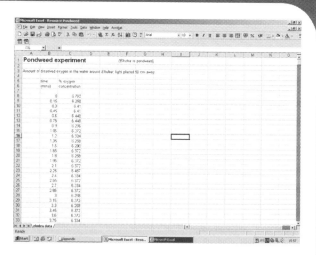

A worked example is provided in the *Teacher-Only Resources* folder on the CD: **Resource Pondweed worked example**.

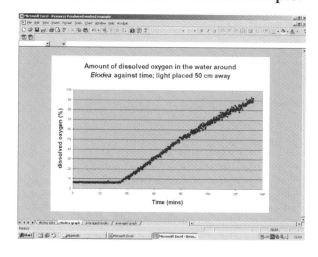

Cross curricular opportunities	
Subject	Programme of study section
Science 1 (investigation)	2g (data logging)
Science 2 (life processes)	3a (logging data using sensors in experiments on photosynthesis)
Science 3 (materials)	2a (data logging)
Geography	5a (logging environmental changes)
	6d (capturing data using a weather station)
PE	4a–d (monitoring heart, pulse, etc)
	7a–c (use video / data logging to record performance levels)